Praise for **Reset with Res**

"The motivation and inspiration that Mandy undoubtedly passes on may very well make the difference during the difficult days ahead, and could have a ripple effect on how history unfolds."
J. WHITE, Naval Information Warfare Center, US Navy

"*Reset with Resilience* is an invaluable resource for anyone who's ever faced challenges on their path to personal and professional success. Having faced my own extreme tests of endurance, I deeply appreciate Mandy's practical, research-backed strategies that not only offer a roadmap for overcoming obstacles but also inspire a profound shift in mindset. Her blend of actionable advice and inspiring real-life examples makes this book a powerful tool for building resilience and achieving your goals. If you're ready to embrace adversity and turn it into your greatest advantage, this book is an essential guide."
COLIN O'BRADY, world record–breaking explorer and *New York Times*–bestselling author

"Mandy masterfully combines personal stories and expert strategies to show you how to transform setbacks into successes. Her empowering message is one we all need to hear."
RIAZ MEGHJI, keynote speaker and author of *Every Conversation Counts*

RESET
WITH
RESILIENCE

MANDY GILL

RESET
with
RESILIENCE

A GUIDE TO GREATNESS

WHEN YOUR GOALS GO SIDEWAYS

PAGE TWO

Cataloguing in publication information is available from Library and Archives Canada.
ISBN 978-1-77458-514-6 (paperback)
ISBN 978-1-77458-515-3 (ebook)

Page Two
pagetwo.com

Copyedited by Rachel Ironstone
Cover and interior design by Fiona Lee
Cover photo by Rhonda Dent
(Styling by Caitlin Buckell and Xoey AxArt)
Interior photos by Sarah Lauze

mandygill.com

To anyone who ever had a dream for themselves.

To my husband, Conor, for believing in mine.
And my parents, Nancy, Bob, Marlene, and Randy,
who raised me to believe that anything is
possible if you commit to it, challenge your fears,
and surround yourself with the right people.

Contents

Introduction
From Small Disasters to Big Success

———————

WOULD LIKE to tell you one of my favorite stories from
back in my radio days.

Even back then, getting up and speaking in front of
an audience felt familiar, comfortable even. Or at least
I thought. And then, in 2010, I was asked to introduce
Rihanna before she came on stage to perform the first Cana-
dian leg of her Last Girl on Earth tour. Rihanna: one of the
most prominent singers of the twenty-first century. This tour
was all the hype, touching down in Europe, North America,
and Australia to support her fourth studio album, *Rated R*.
How in the world did I get asked to introduce her in Vancouver? The request came at the last minute, so I thought maybe
the regularly scheduled announcer was sick or had missed a
flight. I still do not know how I lucked out.

From the moment I was asked, all I could think was that
I may be comfortable talking in front of a camera and a

microphone, but in no shape or form was I ready for nineteen thousand screaming fans. I was twenty-four years old at the time, and as scared and inexperienced as I was, I intended to give it everything I had.

How did I prepare?

I started by realizing that the exhilarating terror I was feeling was probably going to be with me until after I did my part, and I could choose to lean into growth over comfort. I identified my goal–which was acing it on stage so that the whole crowd felt engaged and connected. I planned for success, testing out content and rehearsing every day leading up to the event. I confronted the inevitable hard moments– experiencing doubt and the desire to quit. And because I expected these hard moments, I was prepared for them as well. I breathed through them and refocused on my goal. I visualized the energy and excitement of the audience and how elated I would feel after the fact.

I would love to say that I was cool, calm, and collected on the day of the concert. But the pressure was on, and I was full of nervous energy.

What if I flub? What if I mess up my lines? What if people boo me?

I did my best to keep my composure by arriving at the venue well ahead of time, with close friends who would keep me grounded. One of my girlfriends and I headed backstage to meet Rihanna, who was as kind and sweet as one might imagine, with a beautiful confidence and calm about her. And she was also extremely encouraging.

I could learn from her, I thought. *I'm only on stage for a few minutes, but she'll be there for hours entertaining. I can do this. I can do this.*

When the time came, a crew member directed me to the side of the stage where I would make my entrance. I stood there, facing a big staircase that I would need to climb to get to my spot, and I instantly regretted the long dress I had chosen to wear that evening.

What if it snags on something? What if I get stuck? What if I trip?

On the stage itself, there were huge screens and lights so blinding that I would likely only be able to see the front row of this massive arena.

I was far from a sound studio in a radio station, and it was daunting to say the least.

When the opening act was on their second to last song, the audio team checked my mic to make sure I was good to go. They gave me the thumbs-up, indicating I was ready. I channeled my energy into dancing excitedly on the side of the stage to the band's last song.

The opening act left the stage, and the lights changed. Now I just had to wait for my cue. While I waited, I mentally rehearsed everything I was about to say.

After what seemed like hours but was probably more like forty-five seconds, the moment finally arrived. It was my turn.

I slowly made my way up the staircase, ready to hype up this crowd before the main act. I peered out into the audience, unable to see much but extremely white lights blaring at me. I swallowed and started to speak into the microphone.

What happened next still feels like a nightmare.

With the energy of nineteen thousand expectant fans coursing toward me, my voice fell like a pebble in a giant ocean of space. The microphone was not working.

I stood in silence.

I started to sweat.

And then I panicked.

I was completely unable to control this situation. I looked to the AV team who had double-checked my microphone, squinting enough that I could spot them frantically trying to figure out what was wrong.

I was terrified, frozen.

For weeks I had rehearsed. I had been so prepared for this moment. And there I was, with the reality sinking in that my introduction was not going anywhere close to the way I had intended it to. A technical glitch had thrown off all my plans. For five to ten seconds, I felt that I had sunk into the biggest failure of my life.

And then, mercifully, a question popped into my head: *What Rihanna song will this crowd pick up on quickly and sing?*

The hit "Umbrella" sprang to mind. It had been out for three years at this point. People knew it by heart and above all it was catchy. I focused all my attention on the first and second rows, and in the loudest singing voice I could muster, I sang the signature invitation to stand under this Queen of Pop's *umbrella-ella-ella*. It took a minute to get rows upon rows and sections upon sections of fans up the sides of the arena to join in. Some people in the crowd started the wave with their arms. I kept repeating the line and making eye contact with as many folks in the audience as I could. I was astonished. People were connected, they were having fun, and they were engaged.

To make things even more electric, people raised their phones with the flashlights on. Standing on that massive

Confront the inevitable hard moments—where there's doubt and the desire to quit.

———————

stage, looking out into a sea of glowing lights waving to the tune of "Umbrella," I didn't need the microphone–the energy of this crowd was magic all on its own.

From the corner of my eye, I could see a member of the AV team running to hand me a second microphone. I will never forget the apologetic look on his face. I smiled back, gave him the thumbs-up, and barely needed to say anything into that mic because the crowd was on fire. I was about to hand over this lively stadium to Rihanna in possibly the most creative way she had seen yet.

THE HIGH I experienced after this event lasted for days.

But can you see how, despite all my preparation, the unexpected happened and there was nothing I could do to control it? My plan did not go off the rails because I was unprepared. In a single moment, a technical gaffe tossed all my good intentions and practice into the bin. Perhaps I could have planned for technical failure. And lesson learned about that. But what I learned on the job was how to improvise when things go south. I took the opportunity to get creative and courageous. I decided–and fast–what I was capable of doing to correct the situation. Knowing my goal was to ace it on stage so that the whole crowd felt connected and engaged, I let go of my plans (let's face it, they had been ripped from my hands) and acted in a way that would support my goal.

In your path toward your goal, you are likely to face big, slow detours that happen over time, but a setback can also happen in a flash. Despite all your preparation, the unexpected can and will happen. You could think of it as what makes life interesting. You could think of it as obstacles that put the pressure on you to clarify what you want and your commitment to what you are going for. You could think of it as life generously teaching you to think on your feet, and build confidence and skills as you do.

The takeaway from all this is to–yes, please–prepare and plan for your goal. In the pages ahead, we will talk about all the steps you need to take to identify your goal, visualize it, map it out, recruit your support team, find your motivation and devotion, and act toward that goal.

But, most of all, what I want you to take away from this book is to expect the unexpected. That is, expect setbacks.

A setback is not a reason to quit. It is your opportunity to reset, and with more knowledge, more experience, and more commitment to the things that really matter to you in life.

1

Rip Off
the
Band-Aid

If goals were easy to achieve, you would not need to set them. You would not need to do all the work to support yourself to reach them. You would not really need the focus and effort that you put into important projects. If you feel resistant, you may need to just rip off the Band-Aid and start.

FOCUS DOES not come naturally to most people, especially in today's world where we are being pulled in so many different directions from one moment to the next. Early in my adult life, I started to envision focus as like building a muscle. I had to give anything I was working on the proper time and steps to grow.

Academic pursuits never came easily to me. Fresh out of high school, I attended university to get a bachelor of science degree, but about a year into it I found myself sitting at the dining room table with my mom and dad, who were mulling over my university transcript, saying, "Perhaps it's time to reconsider your career choice." Thankful that I was only nineteen, I still felt the sting of that reality. I did not want to disappoint my parents again. I did not want to disappoint myself. The program was a bad fit. I needed a new direction, a restart, a comeback from the setback.

My parents and I sat for hours at that table talking about what excited me, what I was passionate about. My mom recalled that when I was a kid I never handed in a book report on paper the way the other students in the class did. Instead, I would insist on renting a tape recorder from the 7-Eleven up the street to record my report as an oral story.

With that memory, I felt a rush of energy and the three of us looked at each other knowing this was the path I needed to be on.

Things happened quickly after that. I was accepted into a broadcasting school in a small-sized class.

Not even a month later, on February 11, 2006, my mom, dad, stepdad, sister, and I packed into two cars and, over the course of two days, drove from Calgary, Alberta, to Vancouver, British Columbia. My stepmom stayed back to look after the family dogs. The reality check that came while driving across provinces was quick and real. My family was investing their time in me, and they believed I was capable of achieving great things. I needed to be focused. That was now nonnegotiable.

Within my first week of broadcasting school, a teacher pulled me into his office. He offered what in radio and television we call an air check. This is a form of evaluation in which you listen to a recording of yourself and are given feedback on how to improve and what went well. After this teacher played my clip, we sat in prolonged silence until he finally said, "I need to break it to you. You'll never have a voice for broadcasting."

I was shocked.

I held back my emotions, thanked him for his time, and stormed out of the building. I was not fueled by anger. I was driven by focus, a desire to clear the noise–the self-doubt, the distractions that allowed this instructor's rather harsh proclamation to really rattle me–and to plan for the most successful career I could have ever dreamed of.

Setbacks Are Not Endings

This is a book that lays out a system for you to achieve your goals. By the same token, one of the goals of this book is to show you that setbacks are part of the path to greatness. You can't have one without the other. That is, if you are aiming for something big, whether that means leveling up in your career or pursuing a personal project (launching a side hustle, running a marathon, writing that novel you've had in you for fifteen years ... you get the idea), you are going to face failure at times. Your quarterly targets will fall a little short of the mark. You'll overtrain and strain a muscle. Your main character will get stuck in a room with a locked door that no one has the keys to ... The point is not to let these setbacks derail you.

This book will show you how to set yourself up for success from the beginning and give you the tools you need to carry you through, even when you face challenges.

If you are ready to say what you want and go after it, no matter what setbacks you face, this book is for you.

In the pages ahead, I will guide you through a system for achieving your goals. I draw on my own life experience as an elite athlete, and from working with some of the highest performers in the corporate world and the entertainment industry. I also share a wealth of data from a healthy lifestyle app I founded, Hooked on Healthy Habits, which specializes in behavior change.

You will start by learning to move out of your comfort zone and to act with courage. We will talk about how to identify and clarify your goal, plan for success, and do the work

If I create the
right path for
myself to succeed,
**no one can
break my focus.**

_____

to achieve it. Then you will learn to confront the inevitable hard moments–when you will experience doubt and the desire to quit. I provide strategies for you to overcome lack of motivation and find willpower.

Finally, I offer you a four-step process to correct course after a detour. Because too few of us evaluate our successes to understand just how close we are to achieving our goals, we often see a detour as a failure. But you can reframe a detour as an opportunity to celebrate what worked and figure out what adjustments are required to cross the finish line. This is how you transform a setback into a comeback.

Resilience Is Key

Three months before I graduated from broadcasting school, I was hired by the number-one-ranked rock station to assist on their morning show. Fourteen months later I was hired by a top 40 radio station. Later, I joined the morning show as a cohost, then the afternoon show as a cohost, and then I hosted a weekly television segment on one of Canada's top news stations.

While I was sitting in the studio of the morning show three years after graduation, the teacher who said I would never have a future in broadcasting appeared. He was working down the hall on a sports station and, although we ran into each other occasionally, we never exchanged much more than a "hi" in the hallways. That morning, he walked in, apologized for his early words of discouragement, and congratulated me. I smiled and thanked him.

He had taught me my first lesson in noise. If I created the right path for myself to succeed, no one could break my focus.

Broadcasting was just the start of my career. In 2012, I acquired more education around wellness, investing in school, courses, and more. I built and scaled the Hooked on Healthy Habits app. The idea sparked when radio listeners and television viewers saw the passion in me and wanted coaching to build sustainable habits. Before the app, I had been creating programs in spreadsheets for listeners and viewers who reached out for coaching. As one can imagine, using a spreadsheet was extremely tedious. Back in 2012, the idea of igniting behavior changes via an app felt like a dream. Fast-forward to writing this book, and currently Hooked on Healthy Habits has coached more than ten thousand people to maximize their resilience in the face of rapid change. Before launching the app, I strategically built a team to help me create a personalized system that would equip our clients with foolproof steps to see them reach their ultimate goal.

Examples? A client losing more than two hundred pounds, another client putting on weight to stay healthy and active, still others incorporating the consistent routine of 5 a.m. wake-ups and movement to start the day. Some clients have targeted financial goals, made life-changing nutritional adjustments to produce better blood-panel results and increased energy. Some have run ultra-marathons. Some have been new parents who lost themselves and their routine and wanted nothing more than to feel structure again, to climb to summits they never thought they would be able to thanks to strength training and endurance programming. Some clients desire less screen time and a better focus at work so they can spend more time with family and friends.

Usually, a bad habit or two stands between a person and their goal. Whatever that bad habit is, we catch it, check it, and change it, creating a life-altering experience that lasts. This work through the Hooked on Healthy Habits app has allowed me to acquire one of the world's largest datasets focused on helping people modify behavior to reach their extraordinary goals and dreams, no matter the environment.

I started my own business and became a recognized entrepreneur and CEO while staying involved in broadcasting as a media personality. My commitment to leveling the playing field and opening doors for women across the globe twice earned me Women of Distinction Awards from the YWCA. I have my athleticism to thank for some of my greatest life lessons to date. When I fell in love with sport, I could do only a single push-up from my knees. Through focus, and an underlying joy I felt when I got "in the zone," I eventually began competing and succeeding in the most difficult environments on the planet, from the highest peaks in Nepal to the CrossFit Games competitions to one-hundred-plus kilometer ultra-trail marathons.

I do not tell you this to be boastful. I tell you this because I want you to know that none of it came easily. Setbacks are *always* part of the process in working toward a goal. Deep down I believe we are constantly undermining ourselves on the way to achieving our ultimate goals because we do not understand that setbacks are not endings but part of the path to greatness. I have had so many setbacks on my journey, and what I have learned is that perseverance and resilience are of tremendous benefit to overcoming failure in service to success. And I cannot wait to share this with you.

ACT ON IT

Use a journal to start recording the aha moments from this exercise. Or you can download a free worksheet for your reflections from my website, mandygill.com.

- What bad habits have been standing between me and my goals in the past?

- How have I dealt with unexpected setbacks in the past?

- Am I ready to change this behavior? Why now?

2

Your First Attempt in Living

You have a goal. You know it—*you can feel it*—you are ready to level up. So what's holding you back? To *level up*, you've got to *show up* for yourself. And that requires knowing what distracts you, along with building the courage and willingness for a "first attempt in living" (in other words, a FAIL).

ONE OF Canada's most successful entrepreneurs (and an all-around thoughtful human being) once told me, "If you're making everyone happy, you're not doing it right."

What... say that again? I thought. *Isn't the goal of running a business to make people happy? To give them what they want... so that they can be happy?*

I was starting a meal-prep business, and this person was a mentor to me, but I walked away from that conversation entirely taken aback. Something wasn't sitting right. In fact, I entirely disagreed with what they'd said. Knowing how much I respected them, and recognizing their phenomenal success, I knew I must be missing something.

Not even seven days later, I found myself at the end of a full week and weekend spent with a team of chefs in a commissary kitchen. We were new to this competitive industry, so when customers accidentally forgot to place their orders before cutoff for the Sunday meal delivery, I'd say "no problem." We'd go the extra mile to fill their order, without much time to spare. I'd hustle to do the admin work, and the chefs would scramble to pick up last-minute ingredients. Then it hit me: the exhaustion, the fatigue, the brain fog, the decision paralysis. I was trying to make everyone happy, and in this way not only was I doing the company wrong but I was also forgetting about myself. Why? Because I could not say no, even though we had guidelines in place. I was creating my own noise, my own distractions, and I was losing momentum on short- and long-term goals because I could not stick to what I already knew was essential for success: Knowing when to say no. And showing up for myself.

AS MUCH as showing up for yourself should be an easy thing to do, it seems most of us have forgotten how to do it. Somewhere along the line between childhood and adulthood, our priorities shift to what I'll call false priorities. Activities that distract us. That pull us away from what we're capable of and who we are meant to be. The ones that, deep down, we sense are not serving us and are borderline annoying because they keep us stuck in a "same-old, same-old" routine. Mired in distractions, we live in a foggy state; we overcommit, over-stretch, push the limits of what is best for ourselves, and constantly feel like we are scrambling to keep up. At work and in our personal lives, unnecessary busyness distracts us from achieving short- and long-term goals or, worse, from even starting to work toward them in the first place. Without the tools to identify where and when noise reduction is essential for success, we burn out.

So the question is, How do you effectively prioritize, filter noise, and get ahead with as much energy and collaboration as possible, whether that is in your personal or professional setting? How do you relearn to put yourself first?

I promise, the answer to these questions is not nebulous or elusive. In fact, it is quite systematic. As you work toward a goal, you need to be able to identify when you feel pulled away from it. Then you need to get back to showing up for yourself as promptly as possible. You need clearly defined steps so that this becomes almost automatic, like brushing your teeth or driving a car–something to make coming back from slipups a part of your routine. If you do this often enough, it can become something you don't even have to think of.

But I'm not going to lie. This isn't easy work. It is going to take courage and it is going to take focus and it is going to take a commitment to doing things differently. The first step? Recognizing the distractions.

What Noise?

Distractions from your goal are all around you. Shiny objects like your email inbox, your social media feed, the news, your phone . . . The list goes on. You may not like what I'm about to say here, but it needs to be said: distractions are a great excuse to stay in your own way. What do I mean by that? I mean that you are choosing to pay attention to those shiny objects rather than do the harder work that will advance you toward your goal.

Maybe this is because you do not believe you are capable of something greater, and so a distraction feels comfortable and safe. Maybe it is because you do not realize that your choices are distracting you from your greater vision. Eliminating distractions comes down to you. You can choose first and foremost to recognize that you are worthy of more focus in your life. (Cue the saying "You've got only one life to live, so how do you want to live it?") And you can choose to believe that eliminating unnecessary distractions will bring you toward an abundance of valuable opportunities, quality moments, and perhaps that goal you have always thought was just too far out of reach (really, it's not).

Lastly, maybe you are afraid to fail?

As you start to peel away the layers to look at why you are distracting yourself, you might realize that the prospect of failure feels terrifying, and nearly forbidden. From the time of childhood, we adopt ideas about failure that we carry into our adult years. These messages are spoken or implied by our parents, teachers, or other authority figures. Sometimes observing how people in our life experience and react to failure influences these beliefs. Our personal experiences of failure and the emotional baggage they leave us with also affect our fear of failing.

Failing or Living?

I recently worked with a client who brought up something that really stuck with me. Through years and years of our work together she has had moments of success in showing up for herself; however, she still catches herself "failing" to do so from time to time. Together, we learned to approach a "failure" not as something to be ashamed of, not as a trigger for self-doubt, but instead as an opportunity.

Now, if you are thinking, *Isn't failure the end of opportunities?* I'd like to welcome you to a new outlook, where to FAIL means you have made a "First Attempt in Living."

I'm not saying that changing your entire mindset around failure and conquering it is easy, because it is not. It takes work. What I am saying is that the work is worth it. When you accept the fact that, in some way, you will likely fail in the pursuit of your goal and you consider that failure your first attempt in living, you set yourself up for courage and taking bigger risks than you might otherwise take–including setting your sights on the goal in the first place.

Early in my broadcasting career as a top 40 radio morning show cohost, I was plagued by imposter syndrome. Getting out of my own way didn't seem possible. I was the youngest woman in Canada to ever be hired for such a prestigious position on a station that continuously topped the charts. My colleagues and I woke up a city of more than three million people, every weekday. Was I incredibly talented? Not in the slightest. Did I know that from time to time I was going to fail on air by saying the wrong things? Yes, I went in with eyes open about this. Did I say yes anyway? You bet I did. That saying yes even in the face of sure failure is why I got the job. That, and I was a hard worker. I signed the contract knowing that failure was literally inescapable. All I could control was my own effort to minimize how frequently I failed and how to get myself out of the trap of self-doubt and embarrassment when I did.

Still, it took work.

Every weekday morning, my alarm went off at three. I arrived at the radio station by 3:45 a.m. If you've ever had anxiety on a Sunday before the week ahead, or before an important meeting, you can probably relate to what I felt every morning as I drove to work, ready or not to go live on air. This anxiety lasted for months after I started the job. I intensely desired to be entertaining to a huge audience. I worried about it a lot too. Every morning, as I went through my routine of tying up loose ends before the host, the other cohost, and I headed into the broadcast studio at 5:30 a.m., a wave of fear crashed over me. It was dizzying, paralyzing. At one point I thought something was medically wrong with me. I even went to the doctor about it. But nope. What I was having were stress-induced physical responses because I was putting undue pressure on myself. I needed to do something to shake this.

One Sunday morning, desperate, I headed to a bookstore a few blocks from where I lived. I went straight to the journal section and grabbed the one with the brightest cover, purely with the hope that I would feel joy when I reached for it daily. I decided I would use the journal to try to understand my feelings and why I was having them. I began the next morning. I explored what was pulling me away from myself, my confidence, the trust I had felt when I first knew this position had my name on it. After a few weeks of journaling, I realized that I was so distracted by stories I was making up in my mind that I was sabotaging myself, and my future. I was creating distractions within myself, and I needed to change my thought process.

To do this, I needed a symbol that was going to help me be optimistic and see change through. Optimism, for the most part, is the ability to look at things from a certain perspective where you acknowledge the challenges and still choose to focus on the positive. I needed something to shift my mindset toward energy and motivation, to get over hurdles and achieve what I knew I was capable of. Every morning before the show started, I had to pass through the doorway to the studio, so I thought, *Why not that?* I promised

Distractions are just an excuse to stay in my own way.

_____

myself that as I walked through that doorway I was going to get out of my own way—I wouldn't ignore the fear but would do my best to enjoy my time on air despite it.

Interestingly enough, psychologists coined the term "the doorway effect" and believe that walking through an open door and entering another room creates a "mental blockage" in the brain. It resets memory to make room for a new episode to emerge. For me, each morning when the mic went live to wake up the city, my new episode began. One where I was not going to be disturbed, most importantly not by distractions I had falsely created for myself.

One Day, or Day One?

To reach a goal means you must step beyond what is already comfortable for you. When you consider that, what tends to happen?

Let's look to the example of ultra-trail running.

When I first started running ultras in 2016, I kept myself calm before and during the race with the mantra *I'll sleep in my own bed tonight.* Depending on the elevation gain and descent of the racecourse, fifty kilometers would take me most of the day to run, but the thought of the comfortable, safe, and warm bed that I would return to that night added the extra pep I needed to see myself through any grueling part of the race.

This worked pretty well, until I had a wild idea: tackle my first ever hundred-kilometer race. When I shared this idea with my running coach and my husband, I was sure that they would say I was borderline insane and ask me why

I would even consider doing it. Well, their responses turned out to be the exact opposite: they believed I could do it from the moment the words escaped my mouth. The race I had in mind climbed three mountains, totaling an elevation gain of over twenty thousand feet, and then descending twenty thousand feet too. So now I had a race where there was no hope for me to sleep in my bed the same night. My mental patter had to change.

There was also no way I was ever going to feel fully ready. The race started at five in the morning, with headlamps in the pitch black, and I am certain I barely slept the night before going into the race, purely because of how much I was going to miss the comfort of my own bed.

Here's my point: if you let the thought of discomfort hold you back, growth is slow to happen.

I ran through that entire day, in ninety-degree-Fahrenheit heat. And I kept going (alone) straight through until three in the morning. At the finish line, my husband asked me what I had told myself to keep going. I responded, "It was tougher than I could have ever imagined, but that's what I signed up for."

Waiting to be ready "one day" can take forever. "One day" never comes. But if you start today and make a bet on yourself that you will find a way to get through the tough times (and we will be considering how in the pages ahead), you make today your "day one."

When you commit to your goal knowing that failure and discomfort are inescapable parts of the race to the finish line, you take a stance of resiliency at the starting line. During the hard moments, the belief you have in yourself is put to the ultimate test, and you build character.

Catch It, Check It, Change It

I began a study with clients in the Hooked on Healthy Habits app. Each of them was working toward personal goals of their own, and I asked questions centered around what unnecessary distractions they consciously or unconsciously created for themselves when things felt challenging and uncomfortable. Among those I asked, 82 percent described themselves as experts at creating distractions that kept them from working toward what they wanted most, self-sabotaging on all levels; 74 percent said they had caught themselves at least once daily, over thirty consecutive days, creating an excuse that kept them from working toward what they knew was best for them, and these excuses were based on fear. Looking at this data gave rise to my use of the phrase "catch it, check it, change it." I have my mom to thank for coming up with the creative way of defining this phrase:

- **Catch it** the moment that distractions begin or excuses create a detour for you.

- **Check it** to see if the distractions are nonsense that holds no value of truth and are creating self-doubt about your ability to achieve what you are working toward.

- **Change it**, the actual action, stopping yourself at the start of a distraction or excuse and replacing it with a productive thought or action. Hear yourself say *I'll just go scroll on my phone for a bit before I go out for a jog*, and instead decide to lace up your shoes rather than reach for your phone.

Be honest with yourself and know that by making this conscious decision to create change, new neural pathways are being created in your brain. Distractions become less and less invasive, and excuses are so obvious you can laugh at them from a mile away.

ACT ON IT

Reflect on what stops you from moving forward. Use your journal to record the aha moments from this exercise.

- What distractions and excuses take me off course? (Make two separate lists: one of distractions and one of excuses.)

- What are the alternative thoughts or activities that I will do instead, whenever faced with any distraction or excuse on these two lists?

- When these distractions or excuses show up in my day, can I replace them with a thought or activity that will support what I want in my life rather than detract from it?

3

Choose Courage instead of Comfort

If you are waiting for fear to go away

before you really get started, you're going to be

waiting a long time. A Really. Long. Time. Self-

doubt is nearly universal. But you can learn to

use the quality of courage as a lever to counter-

balance comfort in pursuit of your goal.

T WAS approaching late afternoon. A group of us had just completed a hike from the nearest small settlement and arrived at a tiny base camp made up of eighteen tents for sleeping and one kitchen tent. We had finally made it to the base of Lobuche in Nepal. Over the past week we had climbed to more than five thousand meters above sea level, and I had slowly begun to show signs of acute mountain sickness in the form of a headache and the sound of my heart beating in my ears, even when I was resting. I knew adequate fuel, hydration, warmth, and rest were my best defense to conquer a summit push to the peak of Lobuche (6,119 meters) in seven hours' time.

Knowing that the big climb ahead started with an 11 p.m. alarm to wake us up (because it is safer to climb on snow at night than in the day), my husband, Conor, and I were eager to settle into our tent. But first, we had harness and rope training with our Sherpa, Temba. As Temba showed us what we needed to know for the hike, it became apparent very quickly that the system for rope knots that I had learned prior to climbing in the Himalayas was different from the Nepalese system. I kept reminding myself to maintain a beginner's mindset, but despite all attempts to do so I could not help but question this system. The safety harness I was wearing was a form of protective gear meant to help me avoid injury or death by falling. And the core item of the fall arrest system was a rope. Which, at this point, Temba was adjusting on my waist in a way that was entirely new to me. I inquired about the knots I was unfamiliar with and realized that, because of the language barrier, I was not understanding Temba's explanation. My husband and I spoke no Nepali. Temba spoke more English than the other Sherpas on this expedition, but it was still limited and we communicated mostly through eye contact and head nods. During this half-hour practice on the ropes, I was not going to convince anyone to use my system and I was going to need to trust theirs. This was their livelihood. My life was on the line if anything was tied wrong, and so was theirs.

Then it hit me. I had done a ton of work in my career and life to turn obstacles into opportunities by putting fool-proof strategies into action. One simple strategy is that if you cannot change the obstacle, you change your mindset. I had educated others to do this. Now life was asking me to put that work to the test. I was entirely out of my comfort zone. Far, far beyond it, in fact. And now, more than ever before, I had to put into practice what I genuinely knew to work. I could not let distractions or excuses creep in by even the smallest degree. That alarm was going to go off in a few short hours, and I had to commit to being ready, let go of self-doubt, and let nothing–especially not myself–stand in my way.

After training, we had a quick meal of spaghetti with sauce ahead of what would be a short nap. My stomach full, I stepped through the flapped entrance of the kitchen tent into the night to process my thoughts and, truthfully, my fears. I looked up at the Milky Way and noticed how it lit up the sky. Two words came to me. One was "comfort." The other was "courage." For the next twenty-four hours, I needed to minimize my expectations for comfort and to embrace courage. That would get me to the summit and back down safely.

Between Comfort and Courage

Since that time, I've thought a lot about the relationship between comfort and courage. And I started to conceptualize it using the simple image of a teeter-totter. Imagine it: a long plank with comfort on one end and courage on the other. And what's the pivot point in the center? Fear.

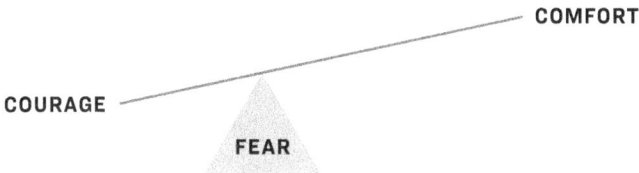

Can you see how the comfort-fear balance illustration shows that fear never goes away? It stands between comfort and courage. Just as I did when I was about to climb Lobuche, you can choose to tip the balance in either direction. If you're moving toward a goal, you likely want to tip the teeter-totter toward courage. The fear doesn't necessarily go away, but if you can put aside your need for comfort, you make room for growth.

When studying the behavior change of clients within the Hooked on Healthy Habits app, I saw that people have breakthroughs and take steps toward the lifestyle advancements they want when they stop letting fear tip the balance more to the side of comfort and instead follow the tilt toward courage. When they consciously became aware of where they were giving too much weight to comfort every day, they started having aha moments. They camouflaged fear with distractions, and those distractions kept them comfortable. Which kept them from growing.

Take Steve, the vice president of a multi-billion-dollar corporation, for example. I was working with him one-on-one, offering him executive coaching. Our monthly focus was for him to face crisis situations in a new way. Rather than reacting instinctively and so often making rash decisions, as was his tendency, he planned to cultivate and maintain a calm state of mind so that he could make deliberate choices. This required him to take a step back in high-stakes situations and pause, breathe, and notice his fear, rather than rush into action as soon as he heard about a problem. He was tasked with looking at adversity through a new lens and *thinking* before acting.

This is a great way to become comfortable with discomfort: pause, breathe, and notice your fear.

When you can see that fear is channeled from facts or emotions that feel uncomfortable to you, you have potentially valuable information. Knowing that gives you a little distance from the fear: you don't need to get unhinged by it. Once Steve and I identified how he needed to reframe certain situations as opportunities for learning and innovation, no longer seeing them as threats, he could turn uncertain situations into ones of hope and possibility. He could recognize the fear and then assess whether he wanted to tip toward comfort or courage, and respond accordingly. That's what you're aiming for.

Facing Failure with Your Head Held High

You may be wondering, in this balance between comfort and courage, what exactly courage is, anyway, and why it matters. Research as reported on in *Psychology Today* identified that some key traits of courage align with other qualities such as conscientiousness, open-mindedness, agreeableness, emotional stability, and resilience. When it comes to courage, actions nearly always outshine mere self-portrayals. To awaken your inner hero in pursuit of your goal, nurture an adventurous, open-minded, and resilient spirit. Embrace calculated risks fearlessly. And–importantly–be open about failure.

In an article in the *Harvard Business Review*, Ron Carucci quoted Microsoft's Chief People Officer, Kathleen Hogan, as saying, "In a culture where people struggle to admit they don't know something, calculating risk can be tricky. Being open about failure helps us balance a growth mindset with accountability. We are learning to not just reward success, but also reward people who fell short while getting us closer. We want it to be acceptable to say, 'I don't know, but I will find out.' Learning from our mistakes gets us closer to our desired results."

It is in moments of discomfort, of stepping beyond what is comfortable, that the best experiences can present themselves.

———————————

I don't know, but I will find out. How powerful would this self-talk be when you are at a crossroads and struggling to find an answer? Or when you are getting back onto the path that will lead you to your desired goal? What if you committed to overcoming failure in service to your success? It would feel great, wouldn't it? So why not start now?

I recently read a *New York Times* article that tells a great story about fear and failure. The article's title, "Want to Thrive? First, Learn to Fail," says it all when it comes to how to build courage. Its author, Jancee Dunn, writes about Sara Blakely, the creator of Spanx shapewear. Blakely and her brother grew up in a household where their father would regularly ask them: "How did you fail this week?" Blakely's father, a proponent of failure without fear, was disappointed if they had no failure to share. Blakely recalls a cheerleading squad rejection greeted with a high five from her dad. Even when she lost a senior class president campaign, her dad celebrated the experience, emphasizing the value of trying. Trained by her father to embrace experiences rather than outcomes, Blakely reflected, "I knew the most popular girl would win, but I did it for the stories and connections."

Living without fear of failure is counterintuitive, it seems, to how most humans are wired. Dr. Amy Edmondson of Harvard Business School notes that our instinct is to evade failure and feel shame when things go awry. Her research explores nurturing a healthy relationship with our mistakes. We can extrapolate from her work to find courage to process our missteps and grow from them. What follows are some steps you can take in this direction.

Contextualize your failures. When you experience failure, you might experience a genuine fear response. Edmondson suggests reframing failures as vital life experiences. You can begin by reflecting:

- What was my initial goal?
- What occurred in reality?
- Can I adjust or take a different path?

Use a journal to write down your responses. This may help you learn and can also be a great record of your growth.

Master the art of adaptation. Instead of getting stuck in post-failure shame, concentrate on ways to move forward or change course. Identify potential pivots and measure success based on progress and newfound knowledge.

Share about your failures. This mindset hinges on humility and honesty. Sharing about your missteps normalizes them and, from an altruistic perspective, it reduces shame about failure for everyone, promotes truthfulness, and facilitates mutual learning.

IT TAKES courage to face your failures with your head held high, and this embodiment of courage can feel as uncomfortable as all get out. But remember, comfort is not what you are going for.

Fear Hack, Life Hack

On the inside of my right arm by my wrist I have a tattoo that reads, "Life begins at the end of my comfort zone." I spotted this saying written on a chalkboard at a farmers' market, of all places, in 2010. It rang so true to me that I wrote it on my mirror in my bathroom. Over time, reading it every day had a profound impact on my outlook on life. I responded to challenges with more enthusiasm, and I started showing up with courage more often, breaking out of the mold of simply doing what was comfortable. It was so powerful that, after two years of reading this on my mirror every time I walked into the bathroom, I wanted to carry the reminder with me everywhere. In 2012 I got the tattoo, and even though the ink has faded now, these words are still a compass for me during moments of decision.

Writing out what you want and adopting the frame of mind that you will face your fears and choose courage over comfort can affect your actions, big time. Within the Hooked on Healthy Habits app, 82 percent of clients say that when they are prompted with a daily task meant to keep moving them toward their goals, they have a much higher success rate. The task can be anything from making a mindset shift (like my tattoo prompt) to doing something physical (for instance, a thirty-minute walk) to setting a work-related boundary (not opening email for the first hour after waking), and countless other examples. What matters is that their capacity is amplified because they're focused. They are less likely to put energy into anything that distracts them from their long-term goal.

My work in national television started as a dream, and I can thank living outside my comfort zone for it. I worked in radio during the time that SiriusXM was gaining traction–Sirius was becoming the new cool kid on the block, offering satellite radio with the option for listeners to choose between more than 150 channels in their car, at home, or anywhere they wanted. On top of that, these channels were commercial free–something local stations like mine that paid salaries with ad sales could not compete with. The usual talk time that we local on-air announcers had was shrinking because we were competing with more music-focused media. I was quickly becoming bored. Radio wasn't feeling very promising as a career, so one day, while longing for that energy I used to share so much more with listeners, I decided to send an email to the vice president of one of the three major national television stations. I asked if he'd be interested in talking about an idea for the morning show television broadcast. And I *volunteered* to do it, *for zero compensation*. The abundance would come from having a creative outlet again.

On the morning of my meeting with the vice president, nerves began to creep in. *Who do I think I am, walking into his office with an idea that could seem so trivial to him? I could cancel, say I was sick . . .* All the regular BS went through my mind. I read the tattoo on the inside of my wrist and walked into his office while holding a binder full of ideas for segments focused on health and wellness. After we exchanged pleasantries and he thoroughly reviewed two of the concepts and the detailed flow of the television segments, he looked up at me and asked, "What are you doing next Tuesday morning?" I was shocked. My eyes must have grown huge as I said, "I'm free all day, except for during my afternoon cohosting hours." He told me I would be on at 7:10 a.m. and to arrive at the television station no later than 6:30. I thanked him for believing in me and promised I would deliver the best health and wellness segment the morning show had ever seen.

The week that followed is one I will never forget. I knew I needed to make this segment shine, but I had no idea who to ask for tips or mentorship. That is, until I was brushing my teeth the night after my meeting with the VP and the photo of Jillian Michaels that I'd cut from a magazine and affixed to my bathroom mirror caught my attention.

At the time, Jillian Michaels was huge for her role on the *Biggest Loser* television show. She was direct and to the point in inspiring people to act. Plus she had such a calm and kind nature. It spoke to me. Hence I had her books, magazines featuring her on the cover... lots of Michaels-created and -related material in my home. The inspirational photo I glimpsed had been there for years.

Someone like Jillian Michaels would be a great mentor. But in this short amount of time how could I find that someone, let alone compel them to respond to my questions and give me guidance from their experience?

Then it hit me.

Jillian Michaels herself was set to be in town on Monday night. She would be at a large theater downtown, speaking, educating, and answering audience questions. How could all this line up so perfectly? I double-checked the date on her website. It was indeed the Monday night before my segment. It was perfect.

I dropped my toothbrush and bought a ticket online. The only seats available were at the back of the theater, but I didn't care. I needed to be in that room to learn something about how she worked her magic.

The next day, I took another step, one that could have received a complete response of no, or no response at all. But I had nothing to lose. I found her publicist's email address online and wrote to them about my segment the day after Jillian's Vancouver tour stop, asking if I could meet her before the show to ask her two questions. I worked ahead, crafting my two questions while awaiting a response. I needed to be direct and concise. If I got a yes, there was no doubt I'd maybe get one minute of Jillian's time. If I got any time at all...

Time passed and my excitement grew, but after days of refreshing my email what seemed like every thirty seconds, I still had no response from the publicist. Monday morning came, and (cue the held breath)... nothing. It had been a long shot, and I was still super excited to see one of my heroes in the flesh, even if it was from row Z.

An hour before I needed to leave for the event, I checked my email one more time. And there it was. A spot in a meet and greet had opened up, and they had given it to me. *Seriously???* This moment still feels surreal when I think about it. And it never would have happened if I hadn't had the courage to simply ask.

I arrived at the venue and followed the directions in the email to get to the meet and greet. With sweaty palms, I stood in line alongside everyone else fortunate enough to meet such an intelligent and inspiring woman. Jillian was about to go on stage and give thousands of people takeaways for showing up for themselves in the betterment of their physical and mental health. I admired that so much. As the line got shorter, and I inched to the front, a thought flashed through my mind: *One day, I would love to share a stage with Jillian Michaels.*

During my one minute with her, I received some of the most valuable information I've ever been given. Despite her stardom, she was empathic to my feelings as a "first timer." We discussed how to inspire viewers and the delivery method to motivate them into action. You could say I had a total girl crush; it was one of the most memorable moments in my career.

The next morning, thanks in part to Jillian's advice, I knocked the television segment out of the park. Emails poured in, compliments came from other departments within the station, and the head producer of the morning show asked me for a meeting. Suffice to say, that was the start of a six-year position with this station as their health and wellness segment host. After that first episode on Tuesday morning, I did one every week, for fifty-two weeks straight. My creativity was in its element.

FAST-FORWARD TO 2018. I was asked to do my first keynote speaking event, at the World Fitness Expo. They wanted me on the main stage in the early afternoon. Even if they had wanted me on at seven in the morning or eight at night, I would have said yes! As flights got booked and details came out about the other speakers, I was speechless to see the running order and the list. I would be speaking in the slot ahead of Jillian Michaels, who was closing the event.

Another "how can this be real?" moment. It was a dream come true. Presenting on stage before her was a total honor, as was the opportunity to thank her for inspiring my journey.

She remembered the day we met, and she asked how the segments were doing. I told her I'd done more than three hundred at that point. We hugged, and I realized that if I had stayed comfortable all those years before I would not have her to thank for the level of success I have had to this day.

The reality is that if you do not try, you will never know what opportunities might open up for you. It is in those moments of discomfort, of stepping beyond what is easy, and perhaps when faced with what seems too good to ever come true, that the best experiences can present themselves. However, you need to take the first step and initiate action for something greater.

ACT ON IT

Answer these questions in your journal:

- What has been keeping me comfortable?

- What courageous traits do I want to strengthen?

- Who do I feel comfortable sharing my failures with?

- Why do I want change?

- What change do I want?

I want to hear from you; please contact me at mandygill.com. Anytime you feel discouraged, or need a reminder of the change you're seeking, visit the website to read other readers' responses and know you're not alone—I am a firm believer that strength happens in numbers. Responses can be anonymous or include your first name and last initial. You never know who else you'll be inspiring as well.

4

Start How You Want to Finish

———

Setting out to accomplish something monumental can make you feel small. At the start you may wonder, *How will it ever get done?* If you give in to worry, you are making the goal that much harder. I have found that a certain mindset is key: go in with confidence, as if you have already achieved what you want.

N o MATTER how big or small the starting lines at which I have stood in my athletic journey, as the clock ticks down the seconds from ten to zero, I always experience the same thing. Everything in me wants to rush out of the gate with all I've got when I hear the gun go off. The energy of everyone around me is contagious— we are all vibrating with excitement and nerves, all at the same time. The competitive edge in me wants nothing more than to achieve what I've set out to do. And I'll admit, it took a lot of experience doing "the start" the wrong way to accept how to do it the smart way.

In running, there is a strategy known as the "negative split," which means you run the second half of a race faster than the first. This requires that, months before the race day, racers establish and implement a pace that charts them toward their finish-time goal. Having a plan also ensures racers are less likely to injure themselves by starting off too fast and fading out along the way. A racer must start with the end in mind, even though the starting-line jitters say, *Go as fast as you can, as quickly as you can, and throw all that strategy out the window*.

Executing the restraint to stick to your strategy takes patience and confidence in the plan; it takes trusting the process. And it takes practice.

Can you think of an area in your life where you have given so much at the start that you burn out along the way? Perhaps you burn out altogether before you are at the end or even the middle of what you originally set out to achieve? If you have, you are not alone. We all do it. We test the limits to see what we're capable of, and that is something never to shy away from. Instead, if you see that the finish line is as important as the starting line, you can care about yourself on an even greater level along the journey. You might ask yourself how you need to prepare, how you need to pace yourself. What obstacles might you face that you can plan for so you don't flame out, thwart your progress, or sabotage your desired results?

In addition to charting the path toward your goal, you can choose to adopt a mindset that will propel you toward what you hope to achieve.

A Star Is Born

You have likely heard the phrase "fake it 'til you make it" a few times in your life. Clichés become cliché for a reason. There's a wisdom to acting as though you have already achieved the goal you are setting out to achieve. This mindset can be a fail-safe for when you encounter obstacles. It is a declaration to the world of what you want and how you are going about getting it. And it can prime you for the experiences you will have when said goal is accomplished.

There is a night during my radio career that I will never forget. As I was reviewing the tightly planned out show for the next day and scanning over what must have been five hundred or more emails that had come in during the day from people who wanted to be on the show, one subject line caught my eye: "We Screwed Up," it read. You could say it was the willingness to admit fault that led me to open the email, and as I did, I quickly caught the gist that a music artist's manager realized they had neglected to get in touch sooner about bringing the artist into the studio. The artist had a show the following night. I responded in my polite yet firm reassurance that the show was planned out too far in advance to allow for spur of the moment drop-ins, and I thanked them for their interest.

I took a sip from the small glass of wine I was enjoying while *The Bachelor* played in the background, and before I even switched from my email back to the show's lineup, the artist's manager had written back. The plea was for any time slot we could make happen for the next day, and the assurance was that we would not be disappointed. I read the email and laughed. *Do people think we just turn on the microphone with nothing planned and we have all kinds of room for extras?* I was irritated by this thought, and I was irritated with myself for starting the conversation with this manager in the first place.

As I took a few minutes to constructively think of how to decline politely–yet again–for some reason, J.K. Rowling popped into my head. She was turned down not by one, two, or three publishers before the Harry Potter series became what we know it to be today. She was rejected more than a dozen times before she finally heard a yes, over a year after she started trying to get published. Maybe it was the sip of wine or maybe it was the optimistic energy radiating from *The Bachelor*, but suddenly I thought, *Who wants to say no to the next best . . . someone?* I revisited the show layout and saw that we could offer the 5:35 a.m. slot.

Now, let me be clear. No one had ever said yes to this slot because it was extremely early and because relatively few listeners tune in at that time. It was the perfect solution–I was offering a slot, but there was no way they would say yes.

Maybe it will come as no surprise at all because of how quickly the manager replied the first time, but about five seconds after I sent the email, I received an energetic "We'll be there!!!"

Great, I thought. *Less than twelve hours before airtime.* How was I going to break the news about this to the host and other cohost?

My palms were clammy when my colleagues walked into the studio the next morning and I delivered the news. They looked at me with disappointment as I handed them a briefing with the name of the artist and their new song, and any other details I could find about this newbie on the scene in an online search. The room was silent. My best guess was we were no longer going to offer the 5:35 a.m. time slot during desperate times. Promptly at 5:15 a.m., the show intern received a call from the artist and her manager to say they were in front of the station.

The studio we broadcasted from could best be described as a fishbowl. A huge window exposed the hallway entrance, and as I sat at my microphone preparing for the show, I saw the artist strolling down the hallway, wearing the thickest bejeweled glasses I had ever seen in my life. She was entirely decked out in makeup and hair that must have taken hours to style, which meant she had been up well before I had. Despite the early morning hour, she was dressed like she was about to go on stage at the Grammys to perform. She was carrying a cane, with a ball of some sort on top, but didn't seem to require it for walking support. It was a prop.

My "I really screwed up" radar went off even louder. What in the world had I said yes to? My coworkers looked at me, still silent. All I could think to myself was, *Let's get this interview done quickly and move on with the show.*

But, from the moment this artist entered the studio, it was obvious that she was going to seize this opportunity with everything she had. The commercial break ended, and she got on the microphone to sing the chorus of her debut song. She sang with the most beautiful, unique voice. The kind that made everyone in the studio perk up with attention. I knew why my instinct said to bring this woman on, even if the last-minute decision was going to land me in the doghouse.

We finished a three-minute interview and thanked the artist and her manager. From behind her thick lenses, she gazed at the three of us and said she had a few extra tickets to her show that night if we wanted to take them. I knew neither of my coworkers would go for a show that started after nine at night. I quickly raised my hand to avoid the awkward silence. She handed me two tickets and thanked us again. As our intern escorted the pair from the building, I looked down at the tickets and realized she was playing nowhere close to where I lived. In fact, it was in an area almost an hour out of the city where no one went after dark. What had I gotten myself into again? All I could think was, *Thank goodness the woman could sing.*

The show was in a pub. A pub where eighteen other people joined us that night. The walls were lined with the artists' posters. It was already way past my bedtime for a weeknight, but as she took the stage, a.k.a. the grimy pub dance floor, she did exactly as she had done in studio that morning: She sang with all her heart, as though she were performing for fifty thousand screaming fans in a stadium. She wore the same thick, rhinestone-bedazzled glasses, cane with the ball on top in hand, and wow could she dance. She had two backup dancers with her, and their energy lit up the dance floor. The small crowd was cheering with excitement in no time.

This artist was starting her career in a way that defined how she wanted it to progress. That morning and evening in 2008, Lady Gaga performed her debut hit "Just Dance" with the same excellence that we would see her perform it to this day. She was not at all famous at that time, but she acted like a star.

What is the lesson for you in all this? You set the tone. If you want to run a marathon but haven't run a race yet, think about how a marathon runner would behave. What lifestyle choices do you need to make? What training and equipment do you need? If you want that promotion, who do you need to speak to? What credentials do you need, and what is the due process in your organization to earn that promotion? Some research may be in order, and the sooner you start behaving the way a person who already has what you want to achieve behaves, the better you set yourself up to become that person.

Start Now

Across the street from the children's hospital in my home-town of Calgary, stood a tiny colorful character home. Up the big set of stairs that led into that home, I was introduced to a therapist who worked with teenage outpatients of eating disorder programs. I was seventeen years old at the time, with a strong belief that I needed to fit a certain mold to be loved. I recall, years before this therapy began, standing with my family in the checkout line of our local grocery store and looking at the magazines merchandised at the cash. One aimed at tweens and teenagers had a big, bold coverline that read, "Once you're skinny you can have it all!" I was young and impressionable. And despite being deeply loved by my family, I had begun to believe that statement to be true. It took years for my battle with anorexia to surface enough for people to ask questions of concern. And frankly I began to be concerned myself. I remember walking up the stairs of an office building where I was interning at the time and feeling faint with every step I took. I was beyond restrictive with my food intake, to the point where if I had six grapes for breakfast instead of five, I struggled to forgive myself. I was malnourished, and I needed help.

In the home of this therapist, I would sit on her cozy couch by the fireplace holding a big white fluffy pillow. During every session, she challenged me to change my unhealthy thinking patterns by making one healthy choice at a time. Several sessions into our work together, she looked at me and asked, "When are you going to start fueling your body so it can thrive?"

Because I was so deep into this hole of disordered eating and depression, I was unfamiliar with what it meant to thrive, and I was stumped about how to respond.

"Monday," I declared. It was Thursday. She looked at me with a stare so deep that I felt I should have had a better answer. But I did not have one.

The room was uncomfortably quiet. Only the sound of the fire crackling in the fireplace filled the space.

"Saturday," I said, feeling a little desperate.

My therapist continued to look at me, silent, while the fire snapped and cracked.

"Tomorrow," I blurted out, pretty much just trying to feed her any answer to dull the discomfort.

She looked down at the pad of paper on her lap where she would make notes, almost as if she was going to write something, but she didn't. She looked back up at me and said, "Why not now?"

I had never thought of that as an option. I was so used to our culture of throwing around phrases like "I'll start Monday" or "That will be my New Year's resolution." But she was right. Why couldn't I start right away?

Sometimes the idea of starting makes us feel uncomfortable, as though all the change needs to be done at once. But as you now know, living in comfort is not a recipe for change and not a good strategy if you want to grow. For some, like it was for me back in that therapist's office, blowing off change with an "I'll start Monday" mentality can feel safer than starting now. But does Monday ever come? What would happen if you made the best decision for yourself toward a better future? If you are waiting, why are you waiting?

Months of deep work, therapy, eating three meals a day, external support, and introspection resulted in my first experience of what it felt like to thrive. In the first few difficult months, when I wanted to divert back to old habits of the eating disorder, every morning I'd ask myself, *Why wait?* Day by day, never diverting from *now*, I was able to climb the stairs without feeling dizzy, and I developed an interest in sports while remaining body positive. I had a renewed purpose in life, and that was to eat to perform. I wanted to fuel myself so I could say yes to any sport, at any moment.

When my career in the broadcast field began, and as years passed, I saw firsthand what media had done to me and my perception of what society and all the pressures to be thin had created in my mind. A drive to be thin, body dissatisfaction, it was all so obvious when I was on the other side of it. Now I had a goal, and that was for no teenager or preteen to ever feel or do the same that I did looking at a magazine, watching a TV commercial, or taking in whatever media source made them think less of themselves. As a broadcaster, grateful sport lover, and recovered anorexic, I became determined to share ways media can complement a healthy lifestyle without the pressures of the so-called shoulds. Because of that moment in my therapist's office when she said, "Why not now?" I have been able to work with youth groups and have seen many aha moments happen for young people when they realize what their bodies are capable of doing when they fuel them for success. I feel so fortunate for that.

You can start now to work toward the smallest or biggest goals you want to achieve in life–why wait?

What Does Your Perfect World Look Like?

There is something incredibly powerful, motivating, and action-orientated about seeing the finish line of a goal. However, you have got to see *more* than the finish line and *way* before it is within your sight. This is seeing your success before it has actually happened. I want to hear how you will feel once you have achieved the goal, how things around you will look, how you will celebrate, and what achieving your goal will change for you going forward. Taking time to visualize this can mean the difference between sticking through the challenges that every big achievement worth having brings and not sticking with the goal at all.

I have had many great role models for leadership throughout my time of working with large corporations; however, when it comes to turning a vision into reality, one leader stands out. You could hear the footsteps walking down a hall and know they were Tracey's without even having to look up. She was tall and confident, caring and concise. Although at times she could be taken as too serious or a bit cold, she had a heart of gold and genuinely worked with the best interests of each of her team members at the radio station where I had begun interning on the morning show. She was hyper-focused and diligent with her time, yet she had an open-door policy for anyone to come in and ask questions or share feedback. I always knew that with Tracey by my side, growth was inevitable.

During a one-on-one meeting, I asked Tracey which questions she felt most inspired her team to act, whether the conversations were about personal or professional objectives.

It takes a lot of experience doing "the start" the wrong way to accept how to do it the smart way.

———————————

As though the answer came right from her core, she responded, "I ask people to consider 'what does your perfect world look like?' and then decide."

I sat there waiting for more, thinking her answer would surely be more complex than this. Tracey smiled and asked, "What challenge do you have in life right now?"

This was an exciting and very complex moment in my life. My career was taking off, and so was my training for what would later be known as the CrossFit Games. (At this time, you were highly unlikely to come across anyone who even knew what CrossFit was.) However, my biggest struggle was that financially things were very tight. As the intern on the morning show, I was earning $33,000 a year. I chalked this up as "paying my dues," but I was living paycheck to paycheck while renting a 450-square-foot studio apartment in downtown Vancouver. I knew feeling this strapped financially wouldn't last forever, and although I could have reached out to my family for help, I wanted to try to make it work on my own.

Tracey knew I arrived at the station before five in the morning, five days a week. And she had seen me running out the door following the show to get to CrossFit training, shortly after ten each day. She could not change the budget for the morning show, but she helped me approach my challenge with creativity by workshopping with me to make my goal more financially stable. She asked me if there was another way I could earn a little more money. On reflection, I saw that, after my exhilarating CrossFit workouts, I still had energy in the afternoons, so I could do something to earn a little more then.

Why hadn't I thought of this sooner?

As luck would have it, although my salary as an intern was set in stone, the station's promotions department did need help. Tracey offered me four hours a day of paid work in that department in the afternoons. Even better, with this new perspective, I realized that most of the roadblocks I was facing were ones I had created myself.

How many times have you said to yourself, "That's too good to be to be true" or "I can't do that," regarding a new opportunity as being out of reach? Once I removed this friction from my thought process, I could visualize the achievement I was working toward as a much lighter, more hopeful, energized, and excited version of myself. I wanted to run toward the goal instead of away from it.

After all this, I couldn't help but wonder why we put these limits on ourselves if the success rate is much higher when we approach life with a "create my perfect world" lens.

During my time competing in the early days of CrossFit Games–dating back to 2010, when local events were called Sectionals–I worked with a visualization coach. We would mentally rehearse winning scenarios, perfecting my technique to achieve a 380-pound deadlift and to overcome obstacles that might happen spontaneously on the competition floor. I can genuinely say this visualization enhanced my performance on the field. Some studies suggest that visualization can also reduce the perceived difficulty of a task. By mentally rehearsing success, you may feel more capable and prepared, leading to reduced feelings of stress or anxiety associated with working toward the goal. Visualization can impact perseverance as well. When you consistently visualize yourself achieving a goal, it can boost your belief in your ability to succeed. This increased confidence can be a powerful driver, pushing you to persist in your efforts and overcome challenges.

When Hooked on Healthy Habits works with clients who want to gain or lose weight, we often have them envision a new wardrobe as a fitting reward. The mental image of slipping into that new pair of jeans, feeling confident and revitalized, acts as a catalyst throughout the journey. Each healthy meal choice and every drop of sweat shed during workouts serves as a testament to the promise of wearing that desired outfit.

While visualizing a reward is not a magical solution and won't replace hard work and dedication, it can be a valuable tool when incorporated into goal-setting strategies. By harnessing the power of your imagination, you can prime your mind for success.

Beyond tangible rewards, simply knowing that your goal has been accomplished offers a unique satisfaction. It is the sense of fulfillment, the quiet confidence that comes with overcoming hurdles and achieving what was once deemed challenging or even impossible. This intrinsic reward holds immense value, fostering a sense of self-belief and pushing you to aspire to even more ambitious goals.

WITH THE Hooked on Healthy Habits app, I had the perfect opportunity to test a mental performance improvement technique that involved "programming" body and mind by visualizing what it would look like to achieve the desired outcome. Here was the process. In one-on-one coaching, coaches would record while clients did the following:

- Chose a specific goal. There was no room to be vague.

- Described what a perfect world would look like–both while they were going after the goal and then when they had achieved it.

The technique was based on the notion that imagined actions activate the same cognitive representation as "actual" actions. What is even more intriguing is that we can learn by way of imagined actions.

When we explained the process of visualization, some clients picked it up easily and others looked at us like they had just seen a ghost. But once they gave themselves freedom to imagine and dream, if you will, with the mindset we all have as children, the floodgates opened, and we coaches could not record their visions fast enough.

Over the course of twelve months of testing, which included weekly one-on-one meetings and daily data recordings done by each client via the app, many of the 218 clients involved reported fewer misses while working toward their goal because energy and time was better served visualizing their goals already happening rather than self-sabotaging with worries or distractions. Further, clients shared their success implementing these mental imagery techniques across different fields, in the workplace or in the classroom.

Once the study was complete, we Healthy Habit folks met as a team and discussed our observations. From an outside point of view, we saw clients show up for themselves, commit to themselves, start how they wanted to finish, and not tomorrow or Monday but *now*, as if it had already happened.

So, again, what are you waiting for? Start visualizing where you want to go and how you want it to be.

ACT ON IT

Refer to the writing you did about change (see "Act on It" in the previous chapter). Choose one thing you would like to change. Now write down your answers to the following questions:

- What is my goal for this change?

- What does achieving my goal look like? (Close your eyes and visualize it before you answer.)

- What does achieving my goal feel like? (Take some time and try to feel this in your body.)

- How will I finish my goal?

- How will I start?

5

Proper Planning

Beats Poor Performance

Whether you like to plan or not, you are going to need some kind of strategy to reach that big dream you have set your sights on. Try this tongue twister: proper planning and preparation prevent poor performance. Every. Single. Time.

N DECEMBER 2021, while Conor and I were boarding a late-afternoon flight to visit family for the holidays, my husband quickly snagged the aisle seat. With a wide grin, Conor stood aside so I could get to the middle seat. The flight was an hour long, and the sun was setting. I was happy to sit closer to the window so I would be able to glimpse one of our favorite views, the Rocky Mountains, from high in the sky. Just as the pilot's voice came over the speakers to announce that we had begun our descent, the sunset hit the mountains in the most beautiful way. I grabbed my phone to take a photo, and the woman sitting in the window seat beside me did the same. We both smiled at each other and enjoyed the moment–less than sixty seconds of otherworldly light on snow-capped peaks. As I put down my phone, I glanced at her book. She asked if I had read it.

The rest was history. We started up a conversation, and before we were at the gate, I learned that her name was Lorraine and she was the president of a highly successful e-commerce company. She asked for my contact information, and a month later I began working with her and her team.

Lorraine had a goal for her company, and there wasn't any time to waste. The organization operated year-round;

however, demand peaked in the fall as the holiday season got underway. Historically, burnout rates had been high during this season–and directly before and afterward. Employees anticipated the demand before it even started, so they were anxious heading into the busy season. This affected everything from productivity to team morale. And afterward, they were tired. The situation was beginning to affect the overall culture at the company. Lorraine wanted a strategy to avoid this cycle of anxiety, overwork, and fatigue during the peak season. The goal was for everyone at the company to a feel positive shift in their professional and personal lives because of changing this pattern.

My role was to examine which self-care processes they could put in place to minimize burnout and increase productivity, performance, and employee retention. To do this, I met each team member and arranged anonymous quarterly surveys to measure burnout. I held in-person burnout education sessions, where we explored the tough conversations needed to normalize temporary burnout but not long-term fatigue. Because the team members were honest about their workload and capacity, the team could start to see how they might better navigate through what had always felt like endless distractions and an overwhelm of tasks to complete. Team members recognized that the old way of doing things had them on a hamster wheel, working ceaselessly to get things done.

In January 2022, we clearly and concisely laid out the roles of each individual on the team and ensured that the organizational chart reflected the levels of leadership and responsibility, then set out to fill any gaps in the work with new hires. A year later, as 2023 began, having put these changes in place, Lorraine sat down with me to discuss the results. This was a few weeks after the company's peak season had wrapped up, and Lorraine reported that her staff had shown an unprecedented level of energy and motivation leading into, during, and following the peak season. She was sure the changes had improved the company's growth and bottom line. I couldn't have been happier about the outcome.

What is the takeaway for you here? This goal had a lot of moving pieces. It was complex and involved multiple stakeholders and business demands. We didn't expect the outcomes to happen immediately, but rather we planned in advance for self-care and resilience strategies for the busy fall season, and we slowly, methodically took the steps to change the systems. We built a high-performing team with a mindset as though we were running a marathon, not as though this was a fifty-meter sprint.

Measuring Backward

Every good plan has a strategy, and through years of experimenting with different approaches, I can tell you that a reverse engineered goal has the highest probability of becoming reality.

What does reverse engineering a goal mean? It means considering what the end product is made of and evaluating how it was built. In other words, to understand how something is made, you need to take it apart, to break it down into its most basic, foundational elements. The steps are:

Step 1: Pick your goal
Step 2: Determine your milestones
Step 3: Set your steps
Step 4: Start the climb

The benefits of a systematic approach abound. You will perceive your goal as more realistic and more attainable and therefore be more likely to work on it. You will know where to focus your energy at any given step toward your goal, while keeping a view of the big picture so that you can adjust your timing and outcomes. When you experience many small wins and gains along the way and learn new skills and abilities, you might just build confidence like a muscle.

The ultimate idea is to ground yourself in the foundational micro and nano goals that make up the larger goal. The great news is that once you know the goal you are working toward, reverse engineering does not need to be overly complicated. Here is the four-step process I have perfected through my work with clients in the Hooked on Healthy Habits app.

Step 1: Pick Your Goal

This first step can feel a bit obvious–it is all about identifying your main goal. It is helpful to do a deep dive into why you have certain goals, and what you expect from pursuing them, to get some clarity. The purpose of this first step is to establish your specific objective and the key motivation behind it. You can ask yourself:

- What is my goal?

- Does it align with my values?

- Is it related to my purpose?
- Why am I pursuing this goal? What is my motivation and vision?
- What is my time horizon for meeting this goal?

So, for example, Lorraine's big goal was to lead a healthier, happier, and more profitable company. When we reflected together, Lorraine said that this aligned with her personal values of self-care and care for others, of family, and of good relationships, and the goal played into her personal purpose as the president of the company to lead a dynamic, energized, and lucrative business. She wanted to create a legacy she could feel proud of and for the influence of her leadership to be felt beyond the employees, to extend to their family and close relationships. She wanted the change in her company to take place within a year. She wanted to reduce symptoms of burnout for all team members by a minimum of 80 percent during peak season, to increase team morale, productivity, and the bottom line.

Step 2: Determine Your Milestones

Another step in reverse engineering your goal is to think backward from the end result, determining the key metrics to measure along the way. This step is best done with a mix of self-reflection on your strengths and weaknesses and how you might improve in areas of weakness, along with research to prepare you for what lies ahead. Here are the questions to answer:

Every
good plan has
a strategy.

- What is realistically required to reach this goal? This could be acquiring new skills, developing better habits, investing financially, etcetera.

- Who has already achieved the goal you want to achieve? Success leaves clues in ways such as changed mindsets or lifestyles, new strategies, and more.

- What was their path? What skills do they have that you do not (yet)? What do they do that you do not (yet)? Listen to podcasts that relate to the goal you are working toward, read books on it, watch documentaries.

- What markers will indicate that you have taken steps toward the goals?

In the case of Lorraine's company, knowing she wanted to mitigate burnout among staff before their next peak season, we looked at other e-commerce companies of her size and scope, how they were resourced, and what wellness practices and benefits they had in place. Lorraine took seminars in leading organizations through healthy change and reached out to a group of peers to gather best practices.

We also looked at what would need to be in place *before* autumn of 2022, and knowing that her team would have to be properly resourced by that time, determined that they would need

- to firmly establish new self-care habits by the end of summer 2022
- to identify gaps in training of and resources for employees by spring 2022

- to complete an audit of the organization's current systems by mid-winter of 2022

Thinking backward showed us that although the timelines were ambitious, with focus and determination, they would be doable.

Step 3: Set Your Steps

Once you've established the core components of your main goal, you need to unpack each component further into actionable steps and tasks. Working forward, you need to think critically and honestly about how you might realistically achieve each goal in step 2.

Leading her organization, Lorraine realized her managers were already time-strapped themselves, so she needed to hire an external consultant (me!) to meet her mid-winter and spring goals. She also needed to plan some additional meetings at the managerial level to strategize for how managers might promote a culture that prioritized employee wellness even in high-demand seasons. We surveyed her team and provided burnout education to all staff as well.

Step 4: Start the Climb

Once you have your goal organized and reverse engineered, it is time to act in small, consistent daily actions. Never underestimate the power of compounding and stacking skills.

Remember step 1, when you defined your expectations? Keeping a reasonable time horizon is crucial for patience and motivation. If you consistently chip away at the steps, you'll eventually reach your milestones, and your goal.

Having decided to address the problem of burnout and staff morale, with my coaching and support, Lorraine took small steps every day to massively shift her organization's culture. The mindset you need for this kind of undertaking is not unlike the kind of training I do for ultra-marathons. What you are setting out to achieve might feel colossal now, but if you do this reverse engineering work, you'll be laying the groundwork for success.

Once you know your plan, the only thing left to do is to stick to it.

Stay the Course

After running more than fifty kilometers and climbing up nearly 2,800 meters (9,186 feet) of desert terrain, it dawned on me: this course would be the biggest and most burly out and back challenge I'd ever encountered. The words "out and back" daunted me most. Staying the course literally became the hardest part of sticking to my plan for this ultra-marathon.

As a trail runner, I'm used to running under a canopy of lush trees on racecourses with finish lines that are different from the starting points. But for this race, there was no tree in sight. The sun thrashed down on us for eight full hours, and the trail conditions were extremely dry, making for loose rocks and quad-burning steep descents that challenged me to find secure landings for my feet. As I approached the half-way point of the race, I took a sixty-second break to bite into the wrap I had packed in my running vest. Suddenly, under the searing heat of the desert sun, every last bit of energy drained from my bones. The brutal, technical route I had taken to get here was the exact same route I needed to face again, only this time in reverse. Second to that, this race didn't offer support crew access, which meant my husband and our dogs, who had traveled with me to this destination race, would not be at any of the aid stations to lift my spirits. After months of training and building hopes and expectations of finishing, the mental and physical challenge felt heavy, impossible.

But I needed to make it back, and the only way back was to stay the course.

When I'm running races like this, and when I'm undertaking any big challenge, I have a simple rule: I can allow one bad thought, but I must not allow two.

Our thoughts, whether negative or positive, gather momentum. Allowing one bad thought? This is not going to kill your dreams. But allowing two? With two negative thoughts, the bad ideas are now gathering steam. So, you notice the first one, allow it, and tell yourself, that is it. Enough.

The rule is simple, but it is not always easy to follow.

The broken windows theory describes something similar. Developed by social scientists George Kelling and James Wilson in 1982, the theory suggests that "visible signs of disorder and misbehavior in an environment encourage further disorder and misbehavior, leading to serious crime." As noted in *Psychology Today*, the broken windows theory "argued that no matter how rich or poor a neighborhood was, one broken window would soon lead to many more windows being broken: 'One unrepaired broken window is a signal that no one cares, and so breaking more windows costs nothing.'" The theory also states that disorder raises people's levels of fear.

Now, passing thoughts are obviously much more ephemeral than windows, whether they are broken or not, and you might not be able to stop a negative thought from slipping through from time to time. But when you need to stay the course to achieve your goal, you cannot afford the luxury of *two* negative thoughts.

When I arrived at that halfway point of the race, it felt like a window had been broken. I knew that if I did not intervene, increasing fear and disorder would follow. Part of my preparation for this race was planning out my own personal "intervention." In this case, I snapped my mind to the mindset of long-distance runner Toby Tanser and his book *More Fire: How to Run the Kenyan Way*. This is a personal account investigating why Kenyans dominate the world of distance running. In the book, Tanser writes, "The Kenyans win because they believe that they can and that they deserve to win." Tanser says that the belief in their own success is manifested in a very humble and non-egotistical manner and that failure simply is not an option. Kenyan runners truly believe that if they put in the hard work and commit to the task at hand and the bigger goal, then they have as good a chance to win as anybody.

Even though I had not signed up to win this race, I had put in the hard work of training for months and months, and I was committed to the goal of seeing through this course.

I threw in one headphone, put on my favorite Luke Combs playlist, and talked enough courage into myself to see the course from a whole new perspective. One dry, cactus-filled, loose-rock footing at a time, I made my way back to where I started. It was a grueling race. The sun continued to pummel me, my legs felt like they were on fire, and I longed to see my husband and our two rescue pups, Potato and Seamus, who ironically loved this dry heat (they were originally from Qatar). I did not give in to any more negative thinking, I just kept my end goal in mind. By the time I got back to the starting line, it had become the finish line, all done up in streamers and balloons. I ran straight into my husband's arms–amazed at what I had just tackled.

ACT ON IT

Work backward versus forward:

- I will accomplish _____.
- When do I want to accomplish this by?
- What are the steps I need to take to make this happen?
- How will I measure this?
- What will I use as positive reinforcement if I find I broke one window, let in one negative thought, and don't want to allow more?

6

Teamwork Makes Your Dream Work

———

The people who are going to help you
"get there," to your goal, are almost as
important as how you get there. Recruiting a
personal support team of people who love
you and a professional support team of
champions will see you through tough moments.
Get the people who have got your back.

M Y PARENTS enrolled me in sport at a young age, and dating back to my earliest memories–playing T-ball when I was four years old–this involvement showed me how much faster we grow by asking a coach, teammates, or parents for support. And by learning to give support to every member of the team. Fast-forward thirty-plus years, and I always find my finger on the pulse of new research on the physical, developmental, psychological, and social benefits of organized sport for children. Being involved in sports helps children learn to control their emotions, channel negative feelings in a positive way, and build resilience.

Adults need these same skills. And you do not have to get them through sports alone. Your colleagues, your community, and even a hobby you enjoy with others might bring you a greater sense of calm, positivity, and connection. Simply put, no matter the size of goal you are looking to achieve, you need people around you who will talk with you about the wins and the losses, and hold you accountable during the easy and the hard days.

When asking people about who will hold them accountable to their goals, I often hear about a little hiccup in their plans: they do not want to "bother" anyone with their goals. Sound familiar? People tend to feel like they are burdening others when asking them for help, support, or simply to check in every few weeks. But the reality is that people want to see you succeed.

Yes, you read that right–people want to see you succeed.

And better yet, they want to be a part of your success. Be bold and ask a few key people in your network to be your "wingman." The worst thing you might hear in response is a no.

When, in advance, you build your dream team of people around you–those who will support you on your way to your big achievement, no matter how audacious, and whether or not the chips are down–you are creating the conditions for success.

You do not have to do it alone. Let's look at the different types of support you might need, starting with personal support.

Personal Support Team

I still recall the moment I hit *send* on a particular email to my running coach, Jerry: "I may be crazy, but I am considering my first one hundred-kilometer trail race. September 10, in place of my fifty-miler. I'm thinking out loud right now... But my thoughts are that this excites me more than traveling for a fifty-miler. Do I sound like I've lost my marbles?"

Jerry, a competitive middle- and long-distance runner since 1986, was quick to reply: "I don't think you've lost your marbles at all. You have a strong capacity for endurance. I have a good sense of what you naturally gravitate toward, and you are definitely what I would call an 'aerobic animal.' You haven't complained once about doing long runs or the increasing general volume of your training. So, why not one hundred kilometers? I fully believe you can do this and run it well as long as we stay consistent and focused throughout the summer. Keep me posted on your final decision, but know that I'm fully on board."

Seconds after I opened Jerry's reply email, I read the tattoo on the inside of my wrist–"Life begins at the end of my comfort zone"–then I headed to the website for the hundred-kilometer race and signed up. Here I was again, ready to take on something I never thought possible for me. However, knowing my dedicated support team–my husband, Conor, and two close friends, Meghan and Dee–would be there in person to crew me at aid stations with fresh socks, snacks, a new layer of sunscreen, and words of encouragement filled me with confidence that I could see this goal through.

Over the months of training that ensued, I did upward of a hundred kilometers a week of running in volume. Many times I called on Conor as my training partner to keep me accountable. I also relied on close girlfriends who joined me for sunrise runs and cheered me on toward my goal. Coach Jerry kept a close eye to make sure I was on track to not be under- or over-trained.

A few weeks before the race, I began to wrap my head around which aid stations I would ask my support crew to attend. After a few days of thinking through the logistics, I received a pre-race email stating that, because of construction and other events in the area, the event organizers were advised that they did not get approval for crew access at more than one aid station throughout the course. If a member of their crew was caught on course outside the one permitted aid station, runners would be disqualified. Also, no pacers (the people who assist marathoners to set their pace during the race) were allowed on course. I was shocked. Not only was I about to run my first one hundred-kilometer trail race, which would mean moving for about twenty hours straight, but I also needed to be prepared to handle my own thoughts–the dark ones–because after a visit with my crew at the thirty-kilometer mark, it would be just me, myself, and I for the next seventy kilometers.

In the forest. Among the bears. Doing my best to stay positive.

I recall hearing that turbulence is an opportunity to lean into the uncomfortable thing. My accountability strategy suddenly needed an injection of creativity. How was I going to stay accountable to what I set out to do, all while feeling the support of my team from a distance? In that remote area of the mountains, relying on cellphone service was not a viable option. And even in the 1 percent chance that I did get a signal, I would want to save my battery charge so I would have my phone in the event of an emergency.

In the days leading up to the race, an idea came to me: letters. I reached out to five people to write me a letter on a piece of paper that I could fold up and place in a waterproof bag to carry in my running vest during the race. How short or long the letter was did not matter. My plan was to pull out a letter any time I felt discouraged, like I was ready to quit. This is how I set myself up for success.

During the race, seventeen hours into running, having covered approximately seventy-two kilometers, I was climbing Blackcomb Mountain in Whistler, British Columbia. It was pitch black on the trail. My headlamp was my only means of light. My stomach had begun to feel queasy, and I wanted to give up. I opened a letter from Conor, which read: "If at any stage you're struggling, compose yourself, gather your thoughts, and formulate your immediate goal to get you through what you're facing. You will succeed. And no matter what, I love you."

I took a deep, calming breath and focused.

It might surprise you that, in that moment, my goal was not to think of the finish line. It was to take one step at a time to get to the top of the mountain and calm my stomach in the process. I realized that for the nausea to pass I needed to stop drinking the fizzy electrolytes that were making my stomach feel bubbly. And I needed to stay calm.

My husband's letter was a reminder to stay focused on the immediate plan, the smaller chunk that would take me closer to the huge goal. It also showed me that reframing setbacks is a key feature of resilience. The bottom line is, your emotional support team should be made up of people who know what you are going after, in increments and overall. They should be people you trust completely, people you know will have your back and deliver you the messages you need to hear when you cannot give them to yourself. Who are those people for you?

Professional Support Team

We all need support within the professional sphere.

Near the end of an hour-long keynote to an audience of over one thousand professionals in the financial space, I prompted a QR code on the large screens and asked audience members to submit the biggest takeaway that they felt ready to act on, beginning now. The responses started coming like a tidal wave while I stood on stage ready to read a few comments out loud. One anonymous responder had written, "As the owner of a business that assists over five hundred high profile clients a year with their assets, I am ready to seek external support. I'm afraid that if I don't, my company, myself, and my beloved team members are going to sink." This individual needed support, and fast. I read the response out loud to the audience, and many heads nodded– they could relate to that feeling, in the moment or at some point in their career. The good thing was that whoever was brave enough to submit this knew they were not alone.

I stuck around after the keynote to take questions from audience members. This is one of my favorite things about events, the intimate time with audience members following their aha moments, when a spark has been ignited, and people are ready for change. A line formed, and after forty-five minutes a single woman remained. Before I could even say hi, she blurted out, "It's me! I'm the business owner who is sinking. My name is Cassandra." Her sweet demeanor, dedication to her clients and staff, and overall plea for help remains one of my most memorable speaking moments. Why? Asking for help is not easy, and I was not going to let her go

The reality
is that people
want to see
me succeed.

_____

about addressing her business's issues alone. Cassandra and I exchanged contact information and organized an executive coaching session for the following week. To see the relief that she felt knowing she would have the support of someone to hold her accountable, to see her through the wins and the losses–it was everything to her. And, I later found out, to her family, who believed so strongly in this mother and leader receiving professional support.

After a year of connecting with Cassandra on a weekly basis, working together to fine-tune leadership, policies, and procedures, we met for an annual check-in. To this day, this incredible woman will tell you if it wasn't for that prompt at the event, and her willingness to share despite being shy to, she wouldn't have the thriving business she has today.

WHILE ATTENDING Harvard Business School's Leadership Program in 2021, I presented a case study on research that revealed that a mere 20 percent of employees feel "their performance is managed in a way that motivates them to do outstanding work." This startled me. For decades I have felt strongly about author John C. Maxwell's quote, "One is too small a number to achieve greatness. No accomplishment of real value has ever been achieved by a human being working alone." If 80 percent of employees do not feel their performance is managed in a way that allows them to do outstanding work, then it is highly likely to see growth in only a minuscule number of employees, let alone companies for that matter.

What do leaders, coaches, or whomever you look to for professional accountability need to know to set you up for success with your goal?

Four key areas serve as a foundation of communication during the launch stage of a new goal. These correlate with how your support team can be best set up for success in long-term performance and to drive you toward your goal. Communicate about this to your team ahead of time.

1   **Shared understanding of the goal's importance.** A shared understanding of purpose equates to a sense of belonging, and ultimately fosters success. When you feel like you are a part of something meaningful and aligned in values together, enthusiasm comes naturally.

2   **Awareness and appreciation radar.** People generally like it when their hard work is recognized and appreciated. Let your support team know how you want to receive feedback. Let them know how you want to recognize any achievements along the way. Perhaps you're someone who wants to celebrate micro moments, or perhaps that steers you off course. You may be surprised how far a few words of clarity and guidance can go to keep one another motivated. After all, this is teamwork.

3   **Healthy and productive debate.** Ensure your support team feels comfortable knowing they can speak up without fear of judgment, that you will provide them an environment that allows them to present their ideas, and you can constructively debate while working through conflict.

4   **Core issues and problem-solving.** Be up front about where you anticipate bumps in the road. What are your non-negotiables that your support team needs to hold you accountable to when moments of turbulence arise?

Before a big race, I make sure my support crew knows how to bring me back to my goal, even if I try to negotiate my way out of it in the moment. For a recent hundred-kilometer race, I told Conor to tell me, no matter how much I wanted to sleep at fifteen to twenty hours in, and no matter how upset I was at the aid station, that I will sleep in a couple of hours but not then. This non-negotiable was set up to help me succeed in a moment when I knew I would feel weakness. My team was prepared to not let me sink.

Non-negotiables can help with small hiccups and big challenges along the way to your goal. Articulating yours to your team will require you to be vulnerable about your own gaps in knowledge and weaknesses. When you trust one another to problem-solve together, you build capacity to respond to unexpected obstacles, strengthening your ability to be adaptable no matter what challenges arise.

Support from a Mentor

Building your personal and professional support team gives you a strong foundation for success; however, one more key position will ultimately bolster your goals. You can be sure there will be stages during the journey of your goal when loneliness creeps in, and your personal and professional support system will do their best to listen, but they may not be able to relate from experience. That is where a mentor comes in. Be proactive and seek one (or more) out.

How imperative is mentorship to your progress? We can learn many things from millennials, and certainly a thing or two on this hot topic. *Huffington Post* reported that 79 per-cent of millennials see mentoring as crucial to their success. And those millennials are 100 percent right.

Here is where the saying "success leaves clues" comes in. To identify who you want to mentor you, take the time to research those who have already done what you are looking to achieve. This can be someone–or several people–who have accomplished your goal, or something close to it. You don't even necessarily have to meet them in person or have direct correspondence with them. Dive into any material that you can get your hands on, from articles to podcasts to books to you name it–there are sure to be hints of struggles along their journey that they will speak of, which can be the make-or-break information you need when times get tough along your path.

My first experience of radio started with a mentor I found, far before university, college, or even halfway through high school. I always loved music, but what I loved even more was the talent the announcers had to segue between songs, and make you feel like you were right in the studio with them. I was intrigued about how they did this with such ease and flow. At fourteen years old, whenever someone asked me, "What do you want to be when you grow up?" the answer at the top of my list was always "radio announcer."

After school and extracurricular activities, I would go home, turn on my radio, and sit in front of it, ready to hit "record" on my cassette tape. Unlike most other kids my age, I was not waiting for my favorite song. No, I was waiting for the announcer to come on. The Calgary station I loy-ally listened to was called Power 107. The announcer I most frequently recorded and played back was named Jonny Staub. Jonny had a unique voice that gave off a caring and compassionate vibe. He was fun and informative. Jonny could weave in and out of songs with smooth ease. My cassette library was full, not of mixtapes but of recordings of Jonny speaking, the seconds before he began, and the seconds after the next song or commercial started up. I would listen again and again. Then I would practice being the announcer and record myself setting up songs–usually by Alanis Morissette and Backstreet Boys–on my boombox. I am sure if someone had found these tapes they would have really questioned what I was doing, but Jonny's talents inspired me, and he became a mentor to me without even knowing it.

Fast-forward to 2008. Two years after I graduated from broadcasting school in Vancouver, fate brought Jonny Staub and me together, at the same radio station almost a decade after I had studied his style. Jonny was midday announcer at the time, and my role on weekends was to go up to various mountains snowboarding with five lucky guests and broadcast from there. Who would be first to volunteer to join every single weekend? Jonny! At one point, I had to admit to Jonny that he had been my mentor, and that my parents' house was still home to stacks of cassette recordings of his on-air material. He laughed, was equally inspired to know he had helped me pave the way to where I got, and the rest is history. Now, I am lucky enough to call my mentor my best friend.

No matter who you research to inspire you, if you reach out to them, you may just hear back and create a new friend with whom you can share the journey of success.

Mentorship goes both ways. As important as it is to have a mentor, it is equally important to be a mentor. Stay open to opportunities when they come your way. You never know how much you may change someone's life, like Jonny did mine, and as I hope to continue doing for you.

ACT ON IT

List your personal and professional support crew and name your mentors. Then answer the following questions:

- How and when will I reach out to each of them with my plan?

- How frequent will check-ins with them be?

- What non-negotiables will I ask them to hold me accountable to? Each member of your team may serve a different purpose for you in this.

Finally, review your goal. Does it still match what you want to do? If yes, continue forward; if not, confirm what your new goal is.

7

Conquering the Seventeen-Mile Dip

Here is the hard news: You will encounter low points as you work toward your goal. There will be tough times and times you want to give up. I tell you this not to depress you but to shore you up, because once you accept the inevitable, you can work with it.

WHEN I'M running an ultra-marathon, I always encounter a moment, reliably at seventeen miles in, when it stops being fun. I call it the seventeen-mile dip. At the starting line, I have all the energy, all the excitement. But at that seventeen-mile mark, I can see that the work needs to be done, and it is tough. This is a dark, lonely moment. And even though I know from experience that I will eventually get through it and make it to the finish line, these little "what if" thoughts creep in and threaten to stop me in my tracks.

We all know that acting tough is different from being tough. When you are heading for something big, something that is taking you out of your comfort zone, you will face moments of fear. (Remember that comfort-fear balance from chapter 3? The fear never goes away, even when–especially when–you are tipping toward courageous action.) You question whether you are prepared enough, strong enough mentally to fight through the hard times. You begin to self-sabotage with excuses or detours.

In all reality, your plans likely will go sideways a handful or more times during the journey of reaching your goal. And if you have an idea in your head about how things are supposed to be, when things do not go as planned, it can be discouraging, frustrating, deflating. These are the moments when resilience becomes key. Because your power is in your response to setbacks.

In one Hooked on Healthy Habits survey, a large majority of clients who worked with us for twelve months or more reported that learning integrative awareness—that is, "being aware of the changing reality in the outside world and how they are responding to it emotionally and physically"—was the best tool for keeping their heads up and staying on course when things got really challenging. Adopting a practice like integrative awareness can help you shift your view so that instead of seeing difficulties as insurmountable, you see that challenges present an opportunity to problem-solve and learn.

Developing integrative awareness takes time. Through the Hooked on Healthy Habits app, we work with people all around the world and in many fields, including, especially, health care and education. People everywhere bring work home with them, and in helping industries, work-related difficulties and challenges abound. The first thing we ask people to do to develop integrative awareness is to step back from what they cannot control, which in itself can be hard to recognize. But in stressful situations that can make you feel emotionally and physically fatigued, even a gentle self-reminder to let go of what you cannot control is a start. For app clients, historically, we have deployed a support team for discussion when difficulties came up. This also meant that the clients were activating their support team, too, for accountability to focus on what was worth putting energy into. Over the course of the twelve months reported on in the survey, the Hooked on Healthy Habits team noticed less time and effort was wasted in the "problem," compared with in the past, and instead time went to the solution, which usually looked like the client focusing on their own self-care to show up for themselves first.

Keep It Simple

Do you trust yourself? Do you trust the process you have established to achieve your goals? Pause and reflect for a few seconds on those questions.

Trusting the process, and above all trusting yourself, can be the hardest part of moving toward your goals, but you will likely find yourself in a place where you cannot move forward unless you do. When you trust yourself and the plan you have put in place, you conserve energy when challenges arise. You need that energy. Not for worrying thoughts or second-guessing yourself but for getting your goal! Consciously conserving your energy is powerful, but being able to do it on autopilot is the ultimate superpower: you react less and might even care less when hiccups arise. How do you do this? Do not overthink it, simplicity is the key to success.

During season two of the *Hooked on Habits* podcast, I asked three clients who had grown with me through the process of achieving their goals in the Hooked on Healthy Habits app to join me for a raw and unguarded conversation about their journeys to success. These three clients wanted more for themselves from a personal health standpoint—more movement, better food choices, and increased mindfulness about how they were treating their bodies. Their achievements included running a first ultra-marathon, confidently keeping up with kids' physical extracurricular activities, and collectively losing nearly four hundred pounds during the time of our work together. In conversations with each of them individually, I asked about the key factor that enabled them to create change, stay on course, and achieve an even greater result than we originally set out for.

Amanda, a busy working mom of three kids was ready to stop dieting and start living. Still to this day she says gastric bypass surgery was the best thing that *did not* happen to her. What was her secret weapon over years of becoming healthier? What made her decide not to go the surgery route or fall back into the trap of an unstable relationship with food like she had developed in her early childhood? Trusting herself. She is not shy to admit it now. In our one-on-one weekly discussions, she genuinely believed she could keep her nutrition in check and follow what we had set out for her to do. But after our calls, she lost trust in herself that she could do it. Admitting the struggle to herself and then opening up to me about it were the first moves in shifting this internal dynamic. Something clicked, and not only was I able to support her on a higher level, but Amanda began to trust herself not to self-sabotage. Having identified the issue, we looked at all the areas Amanda already had trust in herself, to magnify it for this incredibly important area in her life as well. Everything became much simpler. Her energy went to the right places, and in the right direction for her plan.

Darren, an oil rig worker who lived in a camp where it was not uncommon for temperatures to hit minus-forty in the winter, takes change day by day. He was 380 pounds when he first logged in to Hooked on Healthy Habits. He was eating preservative-filled camp food, working long hours, and otherwise living an extremely sedentary lifestyle. To add to it, he was born into an Italian family where food was forever the symbol of love. Changing his routine, setting up his support system, and learning to trust the process of developing a healthy lifestyle took years of taking things "a day at a time," adopting new habits one by one. A routine he painstakingly cultivated he now jokes about: "It's *really easy* if I just follow what you've set out for me to do daily." He keeps it simple; he does not overthink it, and according to his annual medical checkups and impressive recent physical achievements, he is worlds healthier.

I have always highly respected Becky for her grit and ability to show up. She wanted to feel stronger and develop healthier habits. And she came to this goal with a confidence that many of us can learn from. She did not overthink the stuff that most would consider challenging, such as running her first ten-kilometer race or having a number in her head that she wanted to see on the scale that would make her "happy" one day. Instead, she always did the work and laughed lightheartedly on the days that seemed much tougher than others. She kept the hard stuff simple by establishing unwavering routines. She would crawl out of bed at six in the morning to make sure she got a strength workout in, even if she had been up late at a concert the night before. She showed up, and because of that she quickly developed the habits needed to become a stronger version of herself.

Trusting themselves first, taking it day by day, and showing up were the secret "simple" ingredients that propelled

My power is in my response to setbacks.

_____

Amanda, Darren, and Becky to improve their overall longevity and relationship with themselves and others. These habits are like muscles: the more you use them, the stronger they make you.

Get Out of Your Head

"You can't turn around. You're attached to all three of us." I'll never forget those words spoken by Conor while my body was being whipped around from wind gusts of more than a hundred kilometers per hour. Pellets of snow were hitting the little amount of my face I had left exposed, and my footing was anything but secure as we neared the summit of one of the biggest giants in the Pacific Northwest, Mount Baker, standing at 3,288 meters (10,787 feet) above sea level. My husband, a close friend of his from the rescue team he volunteers on, a coworker, and I had started our ascent at midnight, and it was now around eight in the morning. We had worked a full week and gone right into the overnighter to summit. We had been climbing all night in freezing cold temperatures and had just made it up what is called the Roman Wall. Portions of the Roman Wall can be at angles of near forty to forty-five degrees and are sometimes very icy. And there can often be an additional hazard of rockfall from an exposed outcropping above. But the great news is that we had made it up the Wall, and we were only about thirty minutes from the summit of Mount Baker.

Hours before, for extra safety when we were exposed to large crevasses, all four of us had put on our harnesses and roped into one another in a straight line about fifteen feet apart. Despite being attached to one another in this way, my confidence dwindled when the powerful wind gusts could literally pick me up off my feet. The wind was so loud we could hardly hear each other. *This is too much*, I thought. *Why am even doing this?* My breathing sped up and so did my heartbeat. I was panicking.

Without even thinking, I yelled as loud as I could at Conor, who was leading our line. "I want to quit. I'm done."

Conor yelled back to me, "You can't turn around. You're attached to all three of us." He pointed just a few meters ahead to where we would duck in for some relief and then ascend to the summit with a few final steps. Suddenly I realized that if I turned around, everyone turned around.

This was the equivalent of my seventeen-mile dip. And I will be plain with you: it sucked. Every ounce of me felt like I could not continue, but I had come so far, and three other people (who had supported me and were there to keep my feet quite literally on the ground) were relying on me to finish the summit. I needed a mindset shift, and fast.

Immediately I committed to not letting a full negative thought develop. As I took one step at a time toward the summit, I needed to set aside panic and not overthink anything. I had to get out of my own head.

You are going to be okay. You need to stay calm. You need to breathe.

It is incredible what steady breathing and body awareness can do for you in moments of overthinking. I knew what I needed to do, and I was going to do it.

When I breathed and kept my body a bit lower to the ground, the wind had less ability to toss me around. These simple yet profound adjustments allowed me to reach the top of the heaviest glacier-covered mountain in the Cascade Range of volcanoes. And did we ever celebrate at the top– while I sat my whole five-foot-two frame down to stay as low as possible to the ground! A short few minutes to rejoice in reaching the summit, and just long enough for my nervous system to realize that what goes up must go down, and we had a long way to go.

Fourteen hours and fourteen minutes was the total round trip back to our SUV parked at the base of the mountain. Wind burnt, happy, and exhausted, I reflected on how I would have felt if I had quit less than ten minutes before the summit. The thought made me cringe. I would have wasted such a great opportunity because of overthinking and not being logical. I leaned over to kiss Conor and thank him for reminding me to stay the course. He never lets me forget the power of a mindset shift in the toughest of moments.

Sit in It

What happens in that middle phase of change? Most commonly your inner critic takes the stage. We all experience moments where our inner critic takes over and causes us to focus negatively on ourselves; however, if you step back for a moment and observe these thoughts without attaching judgment, then you can start to gain insight about their root cause and begin cultivating a nonjudgmental attitude toward yourself. With self-awareness, compassion, and patience, it is possible to break out of the cycle of judging yourself and make room inside for real growth to get through the middle hump.

The seventeen-mile dip and other such moments are uncomfortable, and as we have talked about, being uncomfortable is not easy. So much so that we reach for everything in our power (even our phones for that extra hit of dopamine) during those moments to get back to feeling comfortable.

Why so much aversion to discomfort?

What do you think would happen if you learned to stay with discomfort?

As my therapist and life coach since 2009 says, "Are you willing to sit in the shit?"

My first answer to that question was, "Certainly not!" So I respect it if that is your answer too.

However, over time, I realized that sitting in the discomfort of situations brings a deeper understanding and desire for a better path forward. Let me give you an example.

In 2018, I spent a day with Wim Hof and his family, learning to get comfortable with the discomfort of cold water therapy. If you are not familiar with the name Wim Hof, you may have heard him referred to as the Iceman. He holds multiple world records for his ability to withstand extremely cold temperatures. He has held himself in ice water for nearly two hours, climbed up to 6,700 meters (22,000 feet) on Mount Everest wearing shorts, ran a half-marathon above the Arctic Circle barefoot, and completed many more feats that will make you wonder if this man is human. I was fascinated to learn more about Hof, and I was grateful to create a long-lasting relationship with his daughters, Isabelle and Laura. We shared a conversation on the *Hooked on Habits* podcast in season two, about how their dad got into his teaching of breathwork and the benefits of cold plunges that have attracted millions of followers throughout the world.

Hof started practicing these techniques at seventeen years old. Years later, he married his wife, and they had four beautiful children together. But then tragedy struck.

As Isabelle describes, "It was like a lightning bolt strike went right through our family." Hof's wife, and his children's mother, died by suicide. Hof was now a single father of four children, ages of six to twelve. The depth of pain the family felt was unfathomable, and yet both Isabelle and Laura said their father managed to be fully there for them and was able to give them his strength and love despite experiencing the hardest time in all their lives. Hof had lost the love of his life and could be found in the backyard of the family home sitting in the cold and doing breathwork to feel his emotions, getting through one moment at a time. Laura said it was these techniques that helped him to sit in his sorrow and pain. He was absolutely defeated, but sitting in the discomfort of cold therapy allowed him to be centered. He used this tool to discover the strength he had within.

Hof's bravery, belief in the benefits of discomfort, and ability to show up for his family by doing the very thing that made him feel most alive—which was breathing his way through—is admirable beyond words. He has worked with universities and research centers all around the world to uncover that frequent exposure to cold is linked to several health benefits, such as reduced inflammation and swelling, improved sleep, better focus, higher energy levels, and improved immune response.

When you inevitably reach a point where you feel like quitting, where continuing to go for the goal does not feel worth the effort and discomfort, remember Wim Hof, who has proved that sitting (or standing) in discomfort is when growth begins.

ACT ON IT

What are three tiny daily actions you can take to advance toward your goal? Write them down in your journal. Keep them simple and easily achievable when things aren't going as planned. Here are some examples:

1 Avoid looking at your phone for the first thirty minutes upon waking. (This ensures that no text message, email, news, etc., will dictate how your day begins.)

2 Meditate for one minute every day.

3 Eat one vegetable with every meal.

8

Forward

Is a

Pace

Sometimes it feels like progress has stalled. During those times when you feel like your steps toward your goal are sized in inches, you can remind yourself that any forward movement, no matter how small, is a pace in the race.

I T WAS during the early morning training hours of a long run before sunrise on a Saturday when a girlfriend of mine, Caitlin, looked at me and said, "I expect it to be hard, but if I'm moving forward that's the only pace that matters. Forward is a pace."

Days before she had signed up for the Death Race, a 118-kilometer race that traverses three mountain summits (nearing 6,000 meters, or 19,685 feet, of elevation gain). I had heard of this event before, and I knew that the race organizers state on their registration forms that even the best runners can succumb to weather that changes from blistering heat to bitter cold and wet, and to not take anything for granted. A year before this I had cheered her on at a fifty-kilometer race, her longest yet, and here she was willing to tackle more than double that in what most would consider highly dangerous wildlife and terrain conditions.

After she told me her thoughts about how she would approach training, I repeated "Forward is a pace" out loud a few times. In the world of running, pace generally refers to how long it takes you to run one mile or one kilometer. But Caitlin's four words suggested a greater truth: if you keep moving forward, you will succeed in the end. So why are humans so quick to judge themselves on how fast or slow they move through things?

Change is hard. And there is no escaping the fact that it involves adusting the usual order of your life and the ways you go about doing things. Generally, you must endure struggle and disorder before order sets back in again. People forget that about the middle phase of change–that this is when the struggle is the hardest. Or they have a false expectation that change will be quick or easy. But if you expect the journey to be hard, you can better prepare yourself for it.

Everyone needs tools to keep them moving forward on their pace during change. I often refer to these as tactics, or "the art or skill of using available means to accomplish an end," as the dictionary defines it. By integrating basic, positive attitudes and beliefs about change and combining them with the right skills, you can learn to adapt in changing situations. Any journey worth taking is rarely straightforward or breezy, at least not all of the time. And like any new activity or function, it can take a while to get used to something new; but over time, and with practice and integration, you can turn a new skill into something you do by rote. In other words, if you keep practicing moving forward, forward movement naturally becomes a pace.

Be patient with the process, trust the process even when it feels difficult, and prioritize consistently showing up. Research shows it can take over two hundred days to form a new habit. Pacing yourself is crucial–the goal is not to exert a heroic effort followed by flaming out. It is to get into a rhythm that builds on itself. Small steps, big gains, because forward is a pace.

Your Language for Success

Humans experience tens of thousands of thoughts per day. We all have familiar internal conversations, but many of us neglect to assess the quality of our self-talk. Even if you are unaware of it, ineffective and unhelpful self-communication will take you to the exact opposite direction of achieving your goal. However, if you consciously improve your self-talk, you can significantly boost your ability to succeed. As noted in *Forbes*, "From a neuroscience perspective, self-talk may be considered an internal remodeling of sorts. However, in order to remodel our brains, we have to change specific words as well. For instance, instead of using the word 'I,' people who use their own name when referring to themselves have better feelings of self-confidence and acceptance. It may feel awkward, but it works."

I learned early lessons from my dad in just how powerful self-talk can be in influencing outcomes. The upstairs floor of the house I grew up in had two bathrooms. One belonged to my dad and stepmom; the other was for me and my sister to share. We would sometimes sneak into their bathroom to use my stepmom's fancy-smelling conditioners. I remember opening my dad's bathroom cabinet and seeing sticky notes on the inside of the door. There were never more than one or two, but they rotated with new "I" statements or quotes on them every week. At some point I asked my dad what they were for, and why these notes changed weekly. His response was filled with confidence and compassion. He said each of these sticky notes held the language that set him up for success. Before AI came up in regular conversations, or even Google for that matter, my dad (with apologies for outing your age, Dad) worked for Philips, helping build out a supercomputer. My dad led and managed large-sized teams in complicated projects with many moving parts and new and latent technologies. No small feat!

So, what did all this mean to my dad? He needed to keep up with a fast-changing and growing company. My dad needed to be on top of his mental game daily to show up and lead a large IT team. He knew that how he communicated with himself was the foundation of it all. Fast-forward a few decades, and I am forever grateful I found those sticky notes and learned this lesson from him—one so valuable that I carry it forward.

How you communicate with yourself—the words of encouragement and the opposite—make things either work for you or against you. This idea is aligned with a core concept of cognitive behavioral therapy (CBT) that suggests that if we can recognize the negative distortions in our thinking patterns, we can re-evaluate them in a more realistic light. The National Science Foundation suggests that 80 percent of our thoughts are negative and 95 percent are repetitive. Health benefits from positive thinking can include better coping skills during difficult and stressful times. My dad's notes on the inside of his cabinet helped him identify positive thoughts that fueled helpful and beneficial reactions to keep moving forward.

Reduce the habit of self-judgment and build a healthy mindset by harnessing and strengthening your language for success. Learn to observe your thoughts with curiosity and compassion; if you want to change the way you feel, then

I don't need to feel
good to get going;
**I need to get going to
give myself a chance
at feeling good.**

———————————

you need to make changes to the way you think. Which, might I suggest, could be accomplished by leaving yourself little sticky-note reminders inside your bathroom cabinet with words of encouragement for how you want to feel, think, and act.

Slow Down to Speed Up

"Why do you think things aren't working for you?" I asked Evelyn, a client new to Hooked on Healthy Habits, during one of our phone calls.

This incredibly hard-working principal, wife, mother, highly involved community member, and honest woman first wrote seeking a big change. Her email read: "I have struggled with my weight and fitness since I was young. I have done extremely well and miserably. I struggle with my eating habits and now I believe it is at a critical point. I am almost seventy pounds overweight, and I have to force myself with all my will just to get out and walk the dogs. I just cannot live like this anymore."

During our call, she explained in more detail, "I'm supporting staff and students all day at work. Cheering on afterschool sports teams. Occasionally putting out fires. And from the time I walk through the front doors of the school before the sun rises in the morning, and until I leave after everyone else has, I am responsible for what does and does not happen in that day. When I arrive home, I'm ready to recharge, and the last thing I want to do is think of what's for dinner. So I've asked my family to plan ahead before I get home. However, if I walk into the house and nothing is prepared, I will eat everything and anything. Anything on the counters, and anything in the cabinets. Usually it's not good, and pretty much empty calories with no real protein or whole food ingredients. Then by the time dinner is ready I'm not even hungry for it, or I overeat out of frustration."

She ran through this again in answer to my question on the phone. I took a deep breath, feeling great empathy for Evelyn's situation, and asked, "Have you ever thought of pausing during these moments?"

Evelyn's response on the other end was silence. I continued, "What if you paused, sat in your driveway in your car for three or four minutes after work before you walked into your home? You could collect your thoughts during this time on how you want to feel, think, and act, regardless of whether a meal is ready or not upon your walking in the front door. You don't want to continue doing what you're doing right now–it's not working. We need to slow you down before you walk in the door, to speed up making the right decisions for your long-term goals."

Again, she was silent for what felt like thirty seconds at least, and then she said, "Now I get it. You're suggesting I respond rather than react. I've been reacting."

The first week that we put this new behavior into action, not every day was easy. In fact, two days Evelyn entirely forgot about the new routine. I reminded her to be kind to herself when she slipped up. It is inevitable to have rough patches; all of us do. Just like she did for everyone in that school, she needed to have her own back. Big self-discipline requires big self-compassion.

Often times, when we are feeling overwhelmed by negative emotions about ourselves or what has gone on in the day (even if it's being nonstop busy), we forget that there is always an alternate perspective available for us to draw upon. In this example, it was the power of pausing and finding strength in changing her thinking patterns. We instilled the strategy to recognize the distortions in her thinking that were creating problems.

If you give yourself permission to slow down and pause for a moment instead of reacting too quickly, you give yourself the chance to recognize that you are well on the way to what you desire. The key here is pausing versus reacting, and doing so before self-sabotaging or allowing negative thoughts to gain power over the situation.

The principle of behavioral activation applies here. Behavioral activation is an important CBT skill that describes how behaviors influence your moods and suggests that engaging in positive behaviors creates more positive emotions. In other words, motivation often follows action. You don't need to feel good to get going; you need to get going to give yourself a chance at feeling good. Even if it means one of your actions is pausing so you can regroup for three to four minutes and show up for yourself, in your best way.

ACT ON IT

What is your language for success to keep moving forward?
Remember that if you want to change the way you feel, then
you will need to make changes to the way you think and act.
In your journal, list five sticky-note-worthy prompts that you
find encouraging; even better, start these prompts with "I"
and stick them where you will see them daily.

9

Make It about a Bigger Thing

———

Just like setbacks are parts of goals,
the qualities of motivation and dedication
are two parts of a whole unit. Motivation is
that spark that initiates movement toward
your end aim. Dedication is the slow-burning
fire that keeps you moving. In other words,
devotion keeps you in motion.

"WE SHATTERED a lot of expectations, even our own expectations," Clayton Marsh, a triplet who was born with cerebral palsy, told me in an interview. Clayton had just participated in the Wildhorse Traverse, a demanding fifty-two-kilometer trail race that winds through stunning canyons, continues along steep technical singletrack, and finishes by passing through vineyards and past waterfalls in the Okanagan region of British Columbia. It also has 1,800 meters (5,906 feet) of elevation gain and 1,900 meters (over 6,200 feet) of descent. Clayton–a vice president on the board of CRIS (Community Recreational Initiatives Society) Adaptive Adventures, a nonprofit that facilitates outdoor adventures for people who experience barriers to getting outdoors–crossed the finish line in eight hours, twenty-five minutes, and thirty-four seconds. His goal? To gain exposure about what is possible for people with disabilities.

Clayton was strapped into a single-wheeled adaptive wilderness chair specialized for the race. Of the seven people on his team, four were running their first ultra-marathon. He was accompanied by five West Kelowna firefighters and two participants from CRIS Adaptive, who pushed and pulled the trail-rider Clayton sat in along all fifty-two kilometers and across the finish line, where I (having also run the race) and hundreds of others with tears in our eyes stood as supporters and witnesses.

Clayton said, "Two of the four training runs we did to prepare for the Wildhorse Traverse had several setbacks. I didn't think we were going to finish the race itself; things weren't going the way we hoped. I was totally prepared for us not to finish, but I was excited either way... We all knew there would be challenges along the way, but we all had the attitude of whatever it takes we'll cross that finish line. We had determination from everyone, and resourcefulness of everyone. We thought of every possible scenario, and it took a lot of planning. Of course, we thought it'd be remarkable if we did finish, and if we were fortunate enough to do so we'd finish right near the cutoff time of ten hours. Well, we crossed with an hour and thirty-five minutes to spare."

Danielle Stalenhoef of CRIS Adaptive, who was a large part of making this dream happen, said, "The ethos of our organization, our mandate, is to say, 'We'll make it possible.' We know and trust that with the right combination of people, experience, and excitement we can do anything. We've learned to find ways to pull things together and make things happen. The time cutoff was our biggest challenge, but we knew anywhere a person can hike and go in the outdoors, this trail-rider can go. We knew we could do it, even if it meant we'd walk through the night to make it happen."

Clayton told me, "One guy, his knees were giving him quite a bit of trouble, and he was determined to cross that finish line, he asked me if we could do this as a team and we slowed right down for him. We ran the last kilometers with him as a team. We weren't going to leave anyone behind. This is the spirit of starting as a team and finishing as a team. As soon as I crossed the finish line, the race director gave me a big hug. We changed people's perceptions. They saw us, and they saw what we can do. We got to show them that it's tough and takes a lot of planning, but with the right mindset we can accomplish a lot."

When I asked Clayton about his next goal, he told me, "This ultra-marathon has fueled my fire to do another one. Maybe have two adaptive athletes next year for a friendly competition. Maybe even do a longer one, or some multiday races. Maybe I'll make a film or enter an adaptive surfing competition. I have yet to decide, but it'll be fun."

Clayton is changing perspectives and making the message about something bigger than himself, every single experience along the way.

Does Motivation Drive Progress?

Often people think they need to rely on motivation as the catalyst for progress. But I have found that motivation will only get you so far. Fueled by your desire and reasons for engaging in a behavior to achieve a goal, motivation provides the initial spark to start a task. But when your motivation flame starts to flicker, when deep down you do not want to quit, but it sure seems easy to, dedication–devoting yourself to a bigger purpose–will see you through.

Motivation and dedication are interdependent. Motivation initiates your goal-setting in the first place, and dedication keeps it on track. Dedication goes beyond a mere desire. It represents your commitment to following through with actions that will lead to the accomplishment of your goal. Motivation is an inner impulse. Dedication responds to that impulse and translates it into hard work. You also elevate your goal to a new level when you dedicate it to something bigger than yourself.

When you ask yourself, "Why does this goal really matter to me?" you are placing yourself at the center, which is all well and fine, and for some even comes naturally. When you look beyond "me," making sure people know they matter to you and inspiring others to act, you set an example about what really matters. What may start out as a selfish pursuit–focusing on others so that you can feel better–will end up a selfless benefit, for everyone. Focusing on the needs of others shifts your thinking. Experiencing compassion, benevolence, and kindness pushes aside the negative emotions. This is one of the best ways to overcome a stressful, unmotivated situation. It makes us feel meaningful in life.

Now you may be saying, "But Mandy, my goal is to get a big promotion so I can afford a nice car, big house, fancy things . . ." Well, that is fine, but fancy things are not *everything*. Attach your goals to a deeper reason. Who, beyond you, will benefit from your achieving your goal? What is your "deeper why"?

This deeper why will drive you when the going gets tough. It gives your goals meaning and purpose. Knowing your why can be the difference between merely wanting something and going out and getting something. Why do you get up and go to work every day? Is it just to make money? Or is it to provide for your family and give your children the best life possible? Maybe you dream of being able to pay for your children to go to college, debt-free. Why do you want to be healthier? Is it to look good? Or is it to live longer, age well, protect your body from illness and injury, and be an inspiration to others?

Now is the time to figure out your why, and who you're doing this for.

Expansive Opportunity

Sometimes in life you will likely reach moments where you are at a bit of a loss, feeling tiny in the grand scheme of things and wondering if that goal you are striving for is worth making a reality (the correct response being, "Of course it is!"). During these moments, you need to look for something bigger than yourself for inspiration and to seek out sources of guidance that help you see beyond your own boundaries and limitations.

While onboarding Hooked on Healthy Habits clients, we ask who they are dedicating this process to (in addition to growing themselves). A working mom, Lorie, came to us striving to strike a balance between her career life and her family life. She knew she needed to change when her daughter, Sabrina, told her it felt like Lorie's work was her number-one priority, and the observation rang true for Lorie. She wanted to put her daughter first, but work had slowly creeped in and taken over, and it wasn't until her teenage daughter alerted her to it that this working mom realized what had happened.

So, she dedicated her goal of finding a work-life balance to Sabrina. Through her daily interactions and choices, she consciously shaped herself into a role model. Recognizing

A deeper why will drive me when the going gets tough.

———————————

that what she did would be more powerful than what she said, Lorie started ending her workdays promptly at five most nights and declining to attend some after-hours work events. She booked dates with Sabrina into her calendar and made sure that, once a month, they did something special on the weekend, emphasizing the significance of family bonds and creating cherished memories together. Even when Lorie had to work outside her regular hours, she deliberately shared the reasons why with Sabrina and made sure her daughter understood that her team leader had negotiated this extra time with her and she was being compensated for it.

By embodying the values she held close, Lorie hoped to inspire Sabrina to become a confident, compassionate, and independent person. She openly discussed her work challenges, highlighting the importance of dedication and commitment. Understanding the impact she had on Sabrina, Lorie molded herself into a role model by embodying qualities and values she wished to impart to her daughter. Their relationship grew stronger. And although finding a good work-life balance remained a struggle, Lorie felt she had more of it, and, importantly, so did Sabrina.

The quest for inspiration beyond yourself is a journey that intertwines the threads of humility and what you need to work on, resilience to stay the course, and staying true to yourself in the process. Whomever you decide to dedicate your goal to, remember that inspiration from something greater than yourself amplifies your capacity for empathy, creativity, and resilience. It showcases the extraordinary strength inherent in ordinary lives.

Greatness is not always marked by grand gestures but is often shown in simple acts of love and compassion, by thinking of one another.

The Numbers Don't Lie

After my best friend's dad was diagnosed with leukemia, she and I signed up for the Ride to Conquer Cancer. This was a 210-kilometer ride that started in Vancouver and ended across the Canada-US border, in Seattle. At the time, I didn't even own a bike, nor had I spent any time on one since my childhood. And despite how much the big objective scared me, supporting a cause that mattered—to my friend, to myself (my grandfather had passed from it), and to cancer research as a whole—meant, of course, I was in.

There's substantial evidence suggesting that participating in charity events or engaging in charitable activities can significantly boost motivation and accomplishment rates. Several studies highlight the positive impact of altruism (the selfless act of helping others without expecting anything in return) and purpose-driven actions on personal satisfaction, motivation, and goal attainment.

When you engage in activities where others also benefit from your actions, you may find your sense of purpose heightened. This is intrinsic motivation in action. That is, something outside you motivates you to act. You might find also that your dedication to the cause leads to sustained effort, and commitment. The emotional connection to the cause fosters a strong sense of dedication and perseverance. For example, engaging in charitable activities provides a profound sense of fulfillment and satisfaction. Research suggests that people who participate in altruistic actions report higher levels of happiness and well-being. This sense of fulfillment can translate as greater determination and drive. Charity events often involve a community or team effort. The camaraderie and social support within these groups create a sense of accountability, encouraging individuals to stay committed and achieve shared objectives. This support network can significantly impact your drive and persistence in reaching goals.

Research conducted by faculty of Griffith University examines the synergy that exists between sport and charity. The study revealed that social affiliation, reciprocity, self-esteem, the need to help others, and the desire to improve a charity of choice contribute to the attachment toward a charity sport event.

What if the goal you're working toward is not an altruistic endeavor? Well, I challenge you to get creative and find a way to get involved and give back in every approach. Let's say you want to travel the world for a year; start researching locations that spark your interest and in which you can also give back to a community or two. This will not only boost your commitment to your goal on a new level but will also motivate you to see it through, all while making a positive impact on others. Maybe you're working toward a promotion. The great news is that networking is an essential part of career growth. Developing the ability to give back while developing yourself may result in your being seen as a high-potential employee who will quickly move up the ladder rather than a high-performing employee who will stay in their current role forever.

Altruistic actions foster motivation, dedication, and a sense of purpose that can positively influence goal attainment. The intrinsic motivation and fulfillment that come from contributing to a greater cause may inspire you to go above and beyond to achieve your objectives within these charitable endeavors. And, hey, why not take a chance to challenge yourself, make new friends, or even just have a great time doing something meaningful!

ACT ON IT

Record your answers to these questions about motivation and dedication in your journal.

- What motivates me to achieve this goal?

- What or who am I dedicating this goal to?

- What do I imagine are the rewards, for me and for others, when I achieve this goal?

10

Detours Become Retours

———————

Too often, failure in one small part of

the goal becomes a detour off the path entirely.

A systematic approach to course correction

turns a potential detour into a retour, where you

recalibrate to your goal with a wider perspective

than you may have even imagined possible.

AFTER TWENTY-FOUR hours of flying halfway across the world, followed by seven days of hiking to an elevation of 4,700 meters (15,420 feet) to acclimatize, my husband and I arrived, euphoric, at Ama Dablam base camp. I was as excited as I was exhausted from the huge trek to get there. The peak of Ama Dablam sits 6,812 meters (22,349 feet) above sea level, and even though it's not the greatest height in the Himalayas, it is a peak known well to anyone who makes the trek to Everest base camp. The striking appearance of Ama Dablam dominates the eastern skyline for several days of the hike.

Climbing it is regarded as a true achievement among the mountaineering community. The technical rock- and ice-climbing skills needed to reach the summit mean you can find even Everest veterans running into difficulty.

A photo of Ama Dablam had been on the fridge at our house back in Vancouver for over six months as we geared up for this adventure. I even had a talented vegan cake artist create a cake in the shape of Ama Dablam–with colorful Tibetan prayer flags and all. You could say Conor and I had visualized this goal in every way possible.

Base camp was buzzing with energy. Conor and I were showed to the tent we would call home during our time here acclimatizing before we would begin to climb to Camp 1, another thousand meters or so higher, and back to prepare for the summit. From Camp 1, whenever a good-weather window presented the opportunity, we would go for a summit push. Over the course of twenty-four hours, we would climb another two thousand meters higher, to reach Ama Dablam's peak. But for now, we were eager to take off our backpacks and rest.

After settling in, we emerged from the tent and looked around in wonder. Sherpas were playing volleyball in a sandpit just a few meters from our tent. In the distance, kitchen staff popped out of the mess tent every so often to feed the yaks. Then I heard the growl and hiss of an espresso machine. *Could this be true? Did I hear right?* We were in the middle of nowhere, in a little village of tents–I must have been dreaming. Being the coffee lover I am, I followed my nose into a large dome tent filled with fifteen or so people laughing and playing cards and sipping fresh coffee. I had found paradise, arguably in one of the most stunning locations in the world. I had a big goal to achieve, and I'd finally made it here to make it reality.

Days passed with making new friends and practicing rope and climbing skills for the exposed and technical climb that awaited. Days were warm, and nights were freezing. I needed two hot water bottles a night for my sleeping bag to keep warm in temperatures that fell below zero Fahrenheit (minus-twenty degrees Celsius). My symptoms of fatigue decreased, and despite having come down with a nasty chest cough, I was feeling good. Things were looking up for what would be the first climb to Camp 1 and back, set for the day before my birthday.

The morning of our climb started with beautiful blue skies. On our way up to Camp 1, we would navigate several ridge lines and massive boulder fields to get to nearly 5,800 meters (19,000 feet) above sea level. I opted for the back of the pack to make sure I took it easy.

At one point, a Sherpa saw me struggling to keep my breath calm. He said, "Slowly." I took a big sigh. He was right. While I was expecting that in two days' time my body would do the hardest thing I'd ever done, my body was the most malnourished it had been in decades because of the altitude and the cough I was experiencing. I needed to slow down. The frustration must have shown on my face because the Sherpa regarded me seriously: "The highest peaks in the world are climbed slowly," he said. I took everything a step slower.

"Slowly" is not a way I'd looked at life in a long time, but there I had no choice. A month before, I could run a hundred kilometers up and down three mountain ranges, but now I was struggling to walk at a slow pace for more than five minutes. My frustration with this drastic change in my body's performance at high altitude was anything but easy to accept. Truthfully, it was the first and only time in my life I can recall my body telling me, "This may be your limit."

Meanwhile Conor was at the front of the pack, and he radiated with excitement for the challenge that awaited. I loved seeing that.

Back at base camp, resting for an even greater adventure ahead, we filled the days with birthday cake celebrations and dancing to Sherpas playing the Tungna, a plucked string instrument made from a single piece of carved wood.

The summit push meant we would start the climb from base camp and go to Camp 1, rest there overnight, awaken early to climb up and pass through Camp 2 to Camp 3, rest for a few hours, and begin again at two in the morning to climb to the summit of Ama Dablam. Then, of course, we would climb safely back down.

If I wanted to reach the top of Ama Dablam, it wasn't going to be quick and easy. This was going to be slow, challenging, and require the most mental strength I'd ever put into anything. When I needed it most, the night before the summit climb, a climber sitting beside me in a frigidly cold food tent said, "You might wear the watch, but we have the time."

The next day arrived quicker than I had wished. My spirits were high, and my symptoms fluctuated. I was willing to celebrate any relief in symptoms at this point! I ate a wholesome breakfast, was fully packed up, and we left base camp for Camp 1.

Five hours later I arrived at Camp 1, where tents perched nearly sideways on rocks. The wind was ripping through the ledge we'd call home for the night, so my husband and I huddled in a tent with numerous others to drink a cup of soup. I felt dizzy and nauseous, and my resting heart rate was 118 beats per minute—very unusual for someone who usually sits in the forties. I did my best to keep my head high and my thoughts positive. I reminded myself this wasn't going to be easy, and I could do it if my body allowed—I just had to keep listening. Mentally, I knew I could get through this with the proper self-talk. Conor and I watched the sunset minutes before five in the evening and curled up in sleeping bags in our tent to keep warm in the minus-fourteen Fahrenheit chill.

I wish I could say I got a good night's rest. I wish I could say I slept well and woke up refreshed and Conor and I celebrated at the top of Ama Dablam in the hours ahead.

Here's what actually happened: After eating a bowl of dal bhat, a Nepalese power dish, and taking a few minutes of gratitude for where we were getting to sleep and what was ahead, restlessness set in. I could hear my heartbeat in my ears and a loud thumping in my chest. My cough returned, sounding deep and echoing in my lungs. It was painful. Conor was trying to sleep, and the last thing I wanted to do was turn this experience into a negative one for the both of us. So I turned to face the direction of the tent walls and tried to calm myself in the pitch dark of the cold night.

Eventually I must have gotten to sleep, because I was startled awake thirty minutes later by Conor saying, "You're not breathing consistently." I was short of breath, and Conor had lain there listening to me trying to get air until he realized it was better to wake me up. My head was pounding, and anxiety was surging through my stomach and chest.

Up until this point, throughout the entire experience in Nepal, I thought I could make it, but suddenly, with little to no sleep and signs of acute mountain sickness worsening, I began to doubt. I quickly quashed the feelings.

I traveled all this way to turn back around? Not in my world.

I tossed and turned the rest of the night until the sun started to rise. Even though I was happy to see light, I was riddled with nerves for what would come next. A decision to continue or not. And if I didn't, I wanted Conor to continue on.

He looked at me, and my cracked lips from the cold, as he said, "Let's get some breakfast in you to see if that changes how you feel."

I blurted out, "If I don't feel better after breakfast when we leave Camp 1, will you please keep going?"

Conor shook his head. "I'll come down with you back to base camp. It's okay—you're not well." Conor is a volunteer on a mountain rescue team back in our home community and is educated on when it's good to continue and when to stop.

Right then, I could see that after the eleven thousand miles we had traveled to get to here, and all our emotional, physical, and financial investment, my goal was not going to become a reality. I was devastated. I wasn't going to make it, at least not that day. But I was determined to convince Conor I was okay to go down by myself and that I wanted to see him make it to the top of Ama Dablam.

Our Sherpa handed us our breakfast through the flaps of our tiny tent. I managed a few bites before a feeling of "I need to get down in elevation in order to get any sense of relief" came over me. It was time. My body made the choice for me. I needed to go. Full of sadness and frustration, I looked up at Conor and told him again how much I wanted him to continue on. I promised him I'd go down slowly and would be waiting for him at base camp tomorrow when he arrived after summitting and descending.

When he finally agreed to keep going, I got chills—the kind that you get when you know something great is about to happen. I was so happy for him to go. I wanted so much for him to experience this.

I choose to show up and persevere, turning pressures into possibilities and strengthening my resilience in the face of adversity, change, loss, and risk.

———————————

Even though I would see him soon, it was one of the hardest but most fulfilling goodbyes I've ever said to Conor.

DID I FAIL at completing the goal of summiting Ama Dablam? Absolutely. Was I sad and frustrated, and did I have so many other feelings of being heavy-hearted? Yes. I had a lot of emotions to process, and a long way down to base camp to experience them. But was I going to let this dip be a detour that took me away from my goal entirely? No. Instead, I practiced a four-step process to course correct and get out of this pitfall. If the failure was a detour, I was going to retour–that is, return to the goal. I was going to take it step by step:

Step 1: Evaluate my success to understand just how close I was to achieving my goal.

Step 2: Celebrate what worked along the way, from the training stages to the actual day itself.

Step 3: Recalibrate to figure out what adjustments I would make going forward.

Step 4: Conquer the next time.

I could keep going with my goal; I just needed to retour to get myself to cross another milestone once I was healed. Let's look a little closer at each of these steps.

Step 1: Evaluate

The first step of the process to course correct was to evaluate my success.

Evaluating your success means looking realistically, from the start of the process to whatever point requires you to evaluate, to see where there were wins. It also means looking for places where you could have done better, not as an exercise in beating yourself up but as an exercise in growth and development.

Many lessons came to me from that hard decision to turn back, the most important being, "you can't control the environment, only the way you react to it." The same principles that lead to success in the world of extreme adventure also apply to everyday settings–in business, in life, and in our communities. We're all climbing peaks (literally and figuratively) and being confronted with changing environments while under pressure. How you choose to show up and persevere in those moments determines the level of resiliency you'll uncover, strengthening the way you look at adversity, change, loss, and risk in all areas of life.

Step 2: Celebrate

The next step in the four-step process to reset after a setback is to celebrate.

Taking a moment to celebrate what went well, despite a failure, or a perceived failure, is a loving act of care for yourself.

In my case, I celebrated that I made it as far as I did in the climb, and that I trusted my body's wisdom to know when to quit.

Step 3: Recalibrate

Recalibrating means adjusting your process to align once again with your goal.

Even during moments when you are staring failure in the face, opportunities are all around you. And you have to be in the right mindset to see them. Neuroscientists have identified a powerful emotion that, when you focus on it regularly, might propel your mind (and body) into an upward spiral: gratitude.

Here are some key aspects of gratitude to be aware of when recalibrating to your goal:

- **Gratitude reduces stress.** According to Dr. Robert A. Emmons, professor of psychology at the University of California, Davis, levels of cortisol (a stress hormone) are 23 percent lower in people who practice gratitude. In challenging moments, practicing gratitude can be a powerful tool to mitigate stress and foster a positive mindset.

- **Gratitude increases emotional well-being.** Studies published in the *Journal of Research in Personality* indicate that gratitude is linked to lower feelings of sadness and higher levels of social support. Embracing gratitude even in tough situations can positively impact emotional well-being, providing a perspective shift that contributes to resilience.

- **Gratitude supports self-leadership.** Cultivating gratitude can enhance personal leadership effectiveness. When people practice gratitude, they tend to experience higher productivity, satisfaction, and more positive relationships. This sense of self-appreciation serves as a personal leadership strategy, fostering motivation and alignment with personal goals, even during challenging periods. Recognizing and expressing gratitude to oneself can be a powerful tool for self-motivation and resilience.

Applying these principles is not just about keeping a gratitude journal at the end of the day but embracing gratitude throughout the day. In challenging situations, ask yourself, "What can I feel grateful for right now, right here?" This activates your brain's ability to find positive aspects, fostering a resilient and opportunity-seeking mindset.

There's no glory in climbing a mountain if all you want to do is to get to the top. The climb itself, in all its moments of revelation, heartbreak, and fatigue, has to be the goal. I did not make it to the summit, but I took many life-changing steps along the way.

Step 4: Crush It!

Once you have evaluated, celebrated, and recalibrated after a failure, the time comes to refocus on your goal. To take this next step, you may need to be adaptable. Circumstances have changed. You might need to let go of old plans and find a new tactic. You might need to exercise emotional control, choosing growth over comfort as you renew your commitment to your goal, which may also involve problem-solving skills, and you might need to tap into your inner wells of strength and positivity. These qualities collectively contribute to a resilient mindset that can serve you well in various aspects of life.

Like most of us, you may have been conditioned to think of situations like my not reaching the summit of Ama Dablam as failure instead of an opportunity. However, once you have started toward something, you are never starting from scratch again in your work toward the same goal. You may have had a setback, and now you are coming back! It is a one-degree shift in your thinking, like turning a thermostat knob.

ACT ON IT

Reflect on a perceived failure in working toward your goal, however slow and big or fast and small. It could be anything from missing a self-imposed deadline to not getting the promotion to skipping a workout day in your fitness goal. Answer the following questions:

- How close am I to achieving my goal, despite this setback? Where have my wins been, and where could I have done better?

- How might I celebrate everything I have achieved toward my goal already?

- Do I still want to achieve my goal? What do I need to adjust as I take my next steps? What am I grateful for accomplishing already?

- What is my next move? How will I conquer it?

Conclusion
Finish Line, Start Line

"**R**ESILIENCE IS built through experience, and in my case, during the hardest loss I will ever experience in my life. There's no way around it. I must live through it." These were the words spoken by a long-time Hooked on Healthy Habits client and close friend while we spent time running in the forest weeks after the unexpected loss of her healthy, academically driven, much-loved-by-all twenty-year-old son. As a heartbroken mom, she spoke these words with such reassurance in the knowledge that life couldn't get harder than what she and her family were currently going through. It's a difficult and an odd compliment to articulate, but I carefully shared with her that I had never in my lifetime witnessed resilience at the level she was living it. The evening of the day her son passed, she reached out. In utter shock, she knew the only way through was support in numbers. We had been working hard toward goals she had set out for herself to achieve over several years at this point, including a race two months later. Healing looked different day by day. But the one thing that remained was her ability to show up for herself for one hour every day, even if the other twenty-three hours felt extremely foggy and dark. Eventually one hour per day progressed to two hours per day of mental, physical, and emotional strength to carry on. I asked her what kept her going, and she responded, "The alternative is not a path I want to go down." I saw perseverance in her eyes when I mentioned there was no pressure whatsoever to take part in the race only weeks away as she planned the celebration of her son's life with her husband, youngest son, and the incredible community that surrounded her. But she said yes to still taking part, without question, knowing that just showing up on the day of meant she had overcome half the battle. Her one request was to call it an "event" and not a "race" to allow her a mindset shift. I will forever be in awe of her ability to show up and to speak up for what she needed from her support crew, not only on the day of the "event" but on every day leading up to it.

You are ready. You have built resilience, and you are more capable than ever before to take on your goal. Resilience, often defined as the ability to bounce back from setbacks, is not just a trait; it is a transformative force that makes you unstoppable. In every area of your life, from personal relationships to professional pursuits, resilience acts as the force that propels you beyond challenges. Resilience, when cultivated and harnessed, becomes a catalyst for unwavering determination and success.

Resilience serves as the psychological backbone that fortifies you against inevitable challenges as you seek to reach your goal. When you are resilient, you refuse to be defeated by setbacks; instead, you view challenges as opportunities for growth. This determination fuels perseverance, allowing you to navigate obstacles with a tenacity that sets you apart in every endeavor, including at work, at home, and in your personal health or fitness goals, or whatever activities you feel the passion to pursue. A resilient mindset not only enhances your problem-solving skills but also positions you as an indispensable asset in the workplace, and beyond.

Resilience is equally pivotal in personal relationships. Interpersonal dynamics inevitably present challenges, but resilient individuals approach conflicts with a solution-oriented mindset. Rather than letting setbacks strain relationships, they use challenges as opportunities for communication, understanding, and growth. This resilience fosters stronger, more meaningful connections. If each challenge becomes a classroom, offering wisdom that shapes your future decisions, then this continuous cycle of learning ensures that your personal and professional development remain constant.

In every facet of life, resilience is the secret sauce that transforms individuals into unstoppable forces. The psychological fortitude, unyielding determination, and ability to learn and grow from adversity make resilience a cornerstone of success. Whether navigating professional challenges, cultivating meaningful relationships, or facing the uncertainties of life, your resilience is the guiding light that propels you forward. Embracing and nurturing resilience is not just a choice; it is the key to unlocking your full potential and becoming truly unstoppable.

Acknowledgments

T HE BOOK you are holding in your hands is the product of my living the system I teach. At many times while in the process of writing the manuscript, going through substantive edits, and even dreaming up the idea, I doubted myself. If it weren't for those I hold close to my heart continuously showing up to remind me how much I was capable of and that it was worth it, even in the hardest of moments, you wouldn't be holding this book and learning from it today.

Upon a return from Nepal in 2022, I said to Conor that I wanted to provide readers with a system and process to reach extraordinary heights in whatever area of their life they desired. Less than ten months later, Conor and I got married in a beautiful ocean-side wedding, on the Sunshine Coast in British Columbia, surrounded by 120 of our best friends and much-loved family members. Writing a manuscript, planning our wedding, training for a hundred-kilometer ultra-trail marathon, all while staying committed to my day-to-day work, proved many times to be the most challenging undertaking in my life to date. Conor's patience, love, and support was a strong foundation at home, along with the check-ins and cheers from my mom (Nancy), dad (Bob), sister (Stacey), stepmom (Marlene), stepdad (Randy), brother-in-law (Hadrian), niece (Elaina), cousins, aunts, and uncles from a distance (Carol M., Craig M., Bob L., Mary L., Caitlyn L., Quinn M., Todd M., Evan M., Koba B., Bob B., Meaghan R., Chris B., Howard G., Diane G., and Cathy D.) made every milestone of this process joyful and memorable. To my sisters-in-law, Sinead (her husband, Malcolm, and their kids, Cathal and Aoife) and Niamh (her husband, Ronan, and their kids, Caoimhe, Eadaoin, Eimear, and Eoin), who never missed a beat from halfway across the world in Ireland to ensure I knew support was coming from them. When I decided to write this book, I started several conversations with my mom stating, "I'm not a good writer." She stopped me each and every time. Telling me I was a great writer, she reminded me to "catch it, check it, change it" whenever I said this . . . and now I always do. Thank you for being a guiding light, Mom.

After speaking to Conor about the idea of making this dream come true, I turned to my friend Riaz M. (another Page Two author) for guidance. During this book's two-year gestation and development–since day one–he has made the time to talk through ideas and roadblocks, and celebrate successes with me. I am forever grateful for his generosity, his belief in this book, and his friendship.

Accountability of writing days began with a 5 a.m. run. Conor would get up with me shortly before and leave for the gym, and my girlfriend Stephanie S. would arrive with her dog, Shira, to ensure my two fur-sons, Potato and

Seamus, got out for an eight to ten kilometer run to start every day. This may not seem important, but it was essential to my day-to-day life, for allowing me to move my body prior to writing at the library, helping me continue training for ultra-marathons, and ensuring our dogs slept well into the afternoon. With zero distractions and full focus, I was unstoppable. Writing accountability sessions were blocked in my calendar with my girlfriend Jamie H. She resides in Upstate New York and was my backbone, listening to ideas and talking them through with me. Whenever my girlfriend Laura W. wasn't educating at the University of Edinburgh in Scotland on children's rights, she was joining me for virtual writing sessions; or better yet, when she'd come home to Canada, she would join me at the library in-person, never missing a beat to offer patience and her expertise. Support was provided unconditionally by my best friends near and far. I can never thank the following individuals enough for their encouragement: Chelsea H., Newsha T., Jonny S., Meghan B., Caitlyn L., Carla B., Christina K., Rosa L., Caity B., Veronica D., Darren M., Kate D., Eric T., Janaan D., Robin B., Carly H., Barry H., the beloved Hall family, Julie Z., Lauren M., Davie O., Joe L., Natasha D., Mimi F., Ian F., Sinead C., Alex C., Catrina E., Katie G., Wade A., Peter M., Angie M., Dave B., Fran P., Owen M., Amy M., Shaina W., James C., Mike R., Emilia D., Marta D., Erin S., Jenny M., Meg W., Jordan U., Amanda L., Amanda W., Nancy Z., Marisa M., Tianna L., Gary M., Chris K., Christine C., Jesse C., Jayde Q., Louis E., Sam C., and, last but certainly not least, Sarina A., for being my right-hand woman in marketing!

To the entire Page Two team, thank you from the bottom of my heart. Start to finish. A genuine heartfelt thank you goes to Jesse F., Kendra W., Marni S., Carmen H., Rachel I., Adrineh D., Louise H., and everyone else who makes up this incredibly talented team.

Many thanks as well to the ImpactEleven community, including the founding partners (Josh L., Peter S., Ryan E., Seth M.), superwoman Ivy G., Jenny D., Jordan B., Connor T., and many more!

To all our compassionate Hooked on Healthy Habits clients who took time during their personal sessions to ask how the process of the book was coming along, thank you. You know who you are!

To the countless speaker bureau agents who believe in the message I share and have a deep sense of desire to spread it by booking me with audiences around the world: Your loyalty and belief in me is appreciated more than I can put into words. This is just the beginning!

These acknowledgments were written while facing Mont Blanc in Chamonix, France, ahead of my husband and my embarking on a 170-kilometer trail run and climbing an elevation gain of over 12,000 meters (39,370 feet) through the French Alps. The trip has included some writing sessions at 4 a.m., and others late into the evening. Conor's understanding of how important to me it is to reach you, the reader of this book, is unparalleled; he has always welcomed my every endeavor with encouragement to follow my dreams. Thank you, forever and always, my love.

Notes

Chapter 2

psychologists coined the term "the doorway effect": Jessica Estrada, "The 'Doorway Effect' Is Why You Forget What You Were Going to Do When Entering a Different Room," Well + Good website, July 9, 2022, wellandgood.com/doorway-effect/.

Chapter 3

some key traits of courage align: Glenn Geher, "What Exactly Is Courage?" *Psychology Today*, September 27, 2023, psychologytoday.com/ca/blog/darwins-subterranean -world/202309/what-exactly-is-courage.

"In a culture where people struggle": Ron Carucci, "How to Actually Encourage Employee Accountability," *Harvard Business Review*, November 23, 2020, hbr.org/2020/11/how-to-actually -encourage-employee-accountability.

that tells a great story about fear and: Jancee Dunn, "Want to Thrive? First, Learn to Fail," *New York Times*, September 15, 2023, nytimes.com/2023/09/15/well/mind/failure-mistakes -advice.html.

our instinct is to evade failure: Interview with Amy Edmondson in Michael Blanding, "Thriving after Failing: How to Turn Your Setbacks into Triumphs," *Harvard Business School Working Knowledge*, September 5, 2023, hbswk.hbs.edu/item /failing-well-2-how-do-you-thrive-as-a-fallible-human-being.

Chapter 4

visualization can also reduce the perceived difficulty: Krista J.
Munroe-Chandler and Michelle D. Guerrero, "Psychological
Imagery in Sport and Performance," *Oxford Research
Encyclopedia of Psychology* online, April 26, 2017, oxfordre
.com/psychology/display/10.1093/acrefore/9780190236557
.001.0001/acrefore-9780190236557-e-228.

we can learn by way of imagined actions: Cornelia Frank, Sarah
N. Kraeutner, Martina Rieger, and Shaun G. Boe, "Learning
Motor Actions via Imagery–Perceptual or Motor Learning?,"
Psychological Research, January 21, 2023, doi.org/10.1007
/s00426-022-01787-4.

Chapter 5

"visible signs of disorder and misbehavior": "Broken Windows
Theory," *Psychology Today*, psychologytoday.com/ca/basics
/broken-windows-theory#.

"The Kenyans win because they believe": Toby Tanser, *How to Run the
Kenyan Way* (Yardley, PA: Westholme Publishing, 2008).

Chapter 6

a mere 20 percent of employees: "Re-Engineering Performance
Management," Gallup Workplace report, gallup.com
/workplace/238064/re-engineering-performance
-management.aspx.

"One is too small a number to achieve": "4 Ways to Intentionally
Win with People," Maxwell Leadership, maxwellleadership
.com/blog/4-ways-to-intentionally-win-with-people/#.

When you feel like you are a part: "Accountability: A Shared Goal
or Purpose," Springtide Research Institute, September 2,
2020, springtideresearch.org/post/miscellaneous/being
-accountable#.

79 percent of millennials see: Julie Silard Kantor, "Four Key Benefits
of Workplace Mentoring Initiatives," *HuffPost*, March 11, 2016,

huffpost.com/entry/four-key-benefits-of-work_b_9432716
?zd_source=hrt&zd_campaign=3728&zd_term=chiradeep
basumallick.

Chapter 7

"being aware of the changing reality": Jacqueline Brassey and Michiel
Kruyt, "How to Demonstrate Calm and Optimism in a Crisis,"
McKinsey & Company, April 30, 2020, mckinsey.com
/capabilities/people-and-organizational-performance/our
-insights/how-to-demonstrate-calm-and-optimism-in-a-crisis.

"It was like a lightning bolt strike": Mandy Gill, "Wim Hof Method:
Laura & Isabelle Hof–Daughters of the 'Iceman'–Tell All
on Changing the Paradigm of Modern Science," *Hooked on
Habits* podcast, March 14, 2022, 1:04:00, mandygill.com
/wim-hof-method-isabelle-laura-hof-hooked-on-habits.

Chapter 8

"the art or skill of using available": s.v. "tactics," *Merriam-Webster*
online, merriam-webster.com/dictionary/tactics#.

but over time, and with practice: "The Change Cycle Overview,"
The Change Cycle, changecycle.com/change-cycle.

it can take over two hundred days: Anne-Laure Le Cunff, "Creating
Habits: How Long Does It Take to Form a Habit?" Ness Labs,
nesslabs.com/creating-habits; Cleveland Clinic, "You Are
Your Brain," Healthy Brains: Brain Facts, healthybrains.org
/brain-facts/.

"From a neuroscience perspective, self-talk": Teri Karjala,
"The Power of Positive Self-Talk," *Forbes*, January 31, 2020,
forbes.com/sites/forbescoachescouncil/2020/01/31/the
-power-of-positive-self-talk/#.

a core concept of cognitive behavioral therapy: American
Psychological Association, "What Is Cognitive Behavioral
Therapy?," APA.org, apa.org/ptsd-guideline/patients-and
-families/cognitive-behavioral.

The National Science Foundation suggests: Charlotte Johnson, "Stuck on Negative Thinking," Care Counseling website, apa.org/ptsd-guideline/patients-and-families/cognitive-behavioral; care-clinics.com/stuck-on-negative-thinking/#.

Health benefits from positive thinking can include: Mayo Clinic, "Positive thinking: Stop negative self-talk to reduce stress," Mayo Clinic: Stress Management website, November 21, 2023, mayoclinic.org/healthy-lifestyle/stress-management/in-depth/positive-thinking/art-20043950.

Chapter 9

participating in charity events or engaging: See, for example, Roger Bennett, Paul James Kitchin, Rehnuma Ali-Choudhury, and Wendy Mousley, "Motivations for Participating in Charity-Affiliated Sporting Events," *Journal of Customer Behaviour* 6, no. 2 (July 2007):155-178, doi.org/10.1362/147539207X223375.

people who participate in altruistic actions report: Stephen G. Post, "Altruism, Happiness, and Health: It's Good to Be Good," *International Journal of Behavioral Medicine* 12, no. 2 (2005): 66-77, greatergood.berkeley.edu/images/uploads/Post-AltruismHappinessHealth.pdf.

The study revealed that social affiliation: Kevin Filo, Daniel C. Funk, and Danny O'Brien, "Examining Motivation for Charity Sport Event Participation: A Comparison of Recreation-Based and Charity-Based Motives," *Journal of Leisure Research* 43, no. 4, (2011): 491-518, nrpa.org/globalassets/journals/jlr/2011/volume-43/jlr-volume-43-number-4-pp-491-518.pdf.

Chapter 10

According to Dr. Robert A. Emmons, professor: Lauren Dunn, "Be Thankful: Science Says Gratitude Is Good for Your Health," *Today*, November 26, 2015, today.com/health/be-thankful-science-says-gratitude-good-your-health-t58256.

Studies published in the Journal of Research: Alex M. Wood, John
    Maltby, Raphael Gillett, P. Alex Linley, and Stephen Joseph,
    "The Role of Gratitude in the Development of Social Support,
    Stress, and Depression: Two Longitudinal Studies," *Journal
    of Research in Personality* 42, no. 4 (August 2008): 854-871,
    doi.org/10.1016/j.jrp.2007.11.003.

About the Author

MANDY GILL, the founder of the Hooked on Healthy Habits app, is a leading expert on building sustainable habits, modifying behavior, and maximizing positive results. As a successful female entrepreneur, CEO, and celebrated media personality, she is a highly sought after keynote speaker, helping organizations to achieve tomorrow's goals while navigating today's distractions. To this end, she has even undertaken work with the US Navy. Mandy shares authentic parallels between the principles she uses to succeed and climbing some of the highest peaks in Nepal and around the world, along with running hundred-plus-kilometer ultra-trail marathons. Mandy builds compelling similarities between the uncontrollable environments in extreme adventure and the ones that we face every day–personally and professionally. Mandy has shared conversations with Lady Gaga and Rihanna while her career was taking shape in the broadcast world. As a Harvard Leadership Program graduate, and published author, she is passionate about leveling the playing field and opening doors for women across the globe, which has twice earned her Women of Distinction Awards. Mandy lives in Vancouver, Canada, with her husband and their family.

Corporate Coaching
for Breakthrough Success

One-on-One Executive Leadership Coaching

Executive coaching is rooted in accelerating an individual's ability to grow strategically and overcome hurdles faster. Through one-on-one executive leadership coaching, individuals will acquire the hard and soft skills necessary to lead first, build as a strong team, and navigate unpredictable situations.

Corporate Leadership Coaching

Let's discuss the strategies and systems that are working, and the ones that require attention to continue growing as a confident, connected team with an unwavering ability to play to strengths and execute accordingly.

The start of our work together begins with creating a deep relationship as a team that understands and executes cohesiveness. As a crucial step in executing a coaching program that aligns with the long-term leadership and culture the company is creating, we will discuss the following:

- Leadership and Management
- Values-Based Decision-Making
- Conflict Resolution
- Giving and Receiving Feedback
- Leadership as an Outflow of Emotional Intelligence

Implementing these discussions is the first step in tailoring an effective leadership coaching strategy for your team, and ultimately allowing each individual in the company to create a greater impact in the lives of customers and clients and on their experiences with the brand. This is done by ensuring that a sustainable performance effort is executed to avoid burnout, loss of productivity, and so on. Throughout our work together, we ensure that the right team members are positioned in the right roles and that they're continuing to grow their education and therefore grow the business. With these systems in place, and a confident foundation of communication and collaboration, your company will experience greater success culturally and financially.

To start your company on this path of resilience and achievement, connect with Mandy directly at **mandygill.com/ contact**.

Invite Mandy
as a Speaker

———————

DO YOU HAVE an upcoming conference or corporate event you'd like Mandy to speak at?

As a sought-after keynote speaker, Mandy Gill helps leaders and their teams thrive in the face of uncertainty in the future of work by strengthening their ability to collaborate, build resilient relationships, and ultimately succeed in ways much greater than they ever thought possible.

In her engaging, thought-provoking, and actionable keynotes, Mandy shares her research from working with clients all over the world. Mandy has perfected the process for helping everyday individuals reach extraordinary goals and results—no matter the environment. Just because the world around us is becoming increasingly busy and distracting doesn't mean that we can't filter through the noise and build our best teams yet.

Connect with Mandy and her booking team directly at mandygill.com/contact.

Ready to
Reach Your Goals?

JOIN ONE OF the world's most effective behavior change apps, Hooked on Healthy Habits, and work with Mandy Gill, alongside her skilled team, to achieve and sustain the healthy habits you've always dreamt of.

The Hooked on Healthy Habits app puts everything you need right at your fingertips to have you feeling your best. You'll be put on a specialized program designed specifically to suit your lifestyle and needs, so you can get the support of weekly virtual consultations to ensure you're on the right track. We will see you through building resilience, modifying behavior, and maximizing positive results.

Mandy and her team can't wait to work with you! Visit **mandygill.com/app** to learn more, and sign up now.

PHOTOS: SARAH LAUZE (A CRIS VOLUNTEER)

Clayton Marsh at Wildhorse Traverse, May 4, 2024.

Breaking Barriers

WERE YOU INSPIRED by the story of Clayton–who was born with cerebral palsy and crossed his first fifty-kilometer trail-race finish line–in chapter 9, "Make It about a Bigger Thing"? Me too!

Scan the QR code below (or go to crisadaptive.ca) to share in the experiences and support more adventures for individuals like Clay to enjoy whitewater rafting, climbing, multiday ocean paddling trips, backcountry hiking and camping, and so on. After scanning the CRIS Adaptive QR code, click the Accessible Wilderness Expeditions program link, where you can send a message to Clay. And if you mention *Reset with Resilience*, they will make sure a donation is earmarked specifically for Clay's future adventures, or possibly for an eventual documentary about him.

www.ingramcontent.com/pod-product-compliance
Lightning Source LLC
Chambersburg PA
CBHW031853200326
41597CB00012B/390